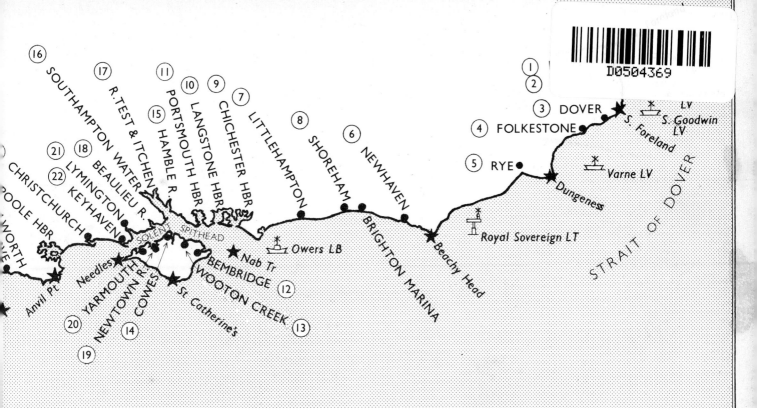

ⓛ

②

③ DOVER

④ FOLKESTONE

⑤ RYE

S. Foreland

LV

S. Goodwin
LV

Varne LV

Dungeness

Royal Sovereign LT

STRAIT OF DOVER

⑯

⑰

⑪

⑩

⑨

⑦

⑮

⑧

⑥

SOUTHAMPTON WATER

R. TEST & ITCHEN

PORTSMOUTH HBR.

LANGSTONE HBR.

CHICHESTER HBR.

LITTLEHAMPTON

SHOREHAM

NEWHAVEN

HAMBLE R.

㉑

⑱

㉒

BEAULIEU R.

LYMINGTON

KEYHAVEN

CHRISTCHURCH

POOLE HBR.

WORTH

Needles

Anvil Pt.

YARMOUTH

NEWTOWN R.

COWES

St. Catherine's

BEMBRIDGE

WOOTON CREEK

㉚

⑭

⑲

SOLENT

SPITHEAD

Nab Tr

Owers LB

BRIGHTON MARINA

Beachy Head

⑫

⑬

LISH CHANNEL

18/17

The Shell Pilot to the

SOUTH COAST HARBOURS

A Shell Guide

K. ADLARD COLES

with plans by
ALAN H. IRVING

FABER AND FABER
3 Queen Square
London

First published as Sailing on the South Coast
Reissued 1939 by Faber & Faber Ltd
3 Queen Square London WC1
Reprinted 1947 (twice)
Second edition 1950 with new title
Pocket Pilot for the South Coast
Third edition 1962
Fourth completely new and revised edition 1968
with present title, reprinted 1971
Interim new edition 1973, with correction pages
This fifth, completely new and revised edition, 1977
Filmset and printed in Great Britain by
BAS Printers Limited, Wallop, Hampshire
ISBN 0 571 04937 0

British Library Cataloguing in Publication Data

Coles, Kaines Adlard
    The Shell pilot to the South Coast harbours. - 5th,
completely new and revised ed. - (A Shell guide)
    1. Harbors - England   2. Pilot guides -
English Channel
    I. Title   II. Series
    623.89'29'422   VK 841

    ISBN 0-571-04937-0

ACKNOWLEDGEMENTS

This book was first published before the Second World War, after which it was followed by revised editions in 1947, 1950, 1962 and 1968. Over the years I have received generous help from very many good friends, to whom I am deeply grateful.

The present new edition has been revised extensively and once again I am indebted to many people for their co-operation, without which my task would have been impossible so great have been the changes, especially while the edition was in preparation.

Firstly, I wish to thank Dr Charles Sergel, with whom I have sailed in his 10-tonner *Sequel* over the past five years, during which he joined whole-heartedly in checking the harbours for my pilot books, including nearly all in this book from Chichester to the Isles of Scilly. I am grateful to Mr D. J. Pooley, who rechecked the harbours from Dartmouth to the Helford River, and to two very experienced cruising friends who visited and provided the information from Ramsgate to Rye. For rechecking individual harbours I am also indebted to Mr John Clarke for Langstone, Mr Eric Roberts for Portsmouth, Mr M. Attrill for Bembridge, Mr R. Fitchett for Wootton, Mr T. Hayes for Exmouth, Mr Stuart Upham for Brixham and other generous helpers. Much assistance has also been received from Harbour Masters to whom I submitted text and harbour plans for independent checking and the latest information about visitors' moorings and facilities. They have been most co-operative and helpful.

The harbour plans in this edition have been drawn by Mr Alan Irving and I cannot thank him too much for his work and for his patience in making literally hundreds of corrections as month by month amendments have poured in from various sources.

Once again I am indebted to the Controller of H.M. Stationery Office and the Hydrographer of the Navy for permission to base most of the plans on Admiralty charts, as also for rates and times of tidal streams from the *Channel Pilot*. Tidal differences referred to Dover have been supplied by the Institute of Oceanographic Sciences or interpolated where not available. Photographs other than my own have been acknowledged under the individual pictures. The brief lists of the launching sites are based on information from Harbour Masters, personal observation and the booklet *Getting Afloat*. I recommend this publication to yachtsmen who make a practice of towing their boats and want to know all the launching sites in Great Britain and Ireland. It can be obtained from Link House, Dingwall Avenue, Croydon, CR9 2TA.

CONTENTS

PREFACE

In this fifth edition of *The Shell Pilot to the South Coast Harbours* the type has been completely reset and this has afforded the opportunity to rewrite the whole book as well as to bring it up-to-date. The harbour plans have all been redrawn and reproduced in a larger size, which improves their clarity. Charted depths and drying heights have been expressed in metres.

However, the fundamental difference between this edition and the earlier ones lies in the reduction of chart datum to the level of LAT (lowest astronomical tide) which for practical purposes may be taken as the level of the lowest predicted tide. As this rarely occurs it presents a superficially pessimistic view showing many minor channels, navigable by shoal draught craft at other states of the tide, as drying or nearly drying out. To correct this, tidal data for each harbour have been improved in this edition by the inclusion of the differences which can be added to charted depths at MHWS, MLWS, MHWN and MLWN, as referred to on page 13. In particular it will be noted that at MLWN in many harbours there may be as much as 1m8 (6 ft) more water than shown on the plans at LAT datum. This makes all the difference when sailing in shoal waters.

Another point which has received attention is the problem of the crowded harbours of today, where it is often difficult to find somewhere to bring up on arrival and especially so at the peak of the season. Every effort has been made to obtain the latest information on the subject of anchorages available, marina berths and visitors' moorings. The latter have been improved in many West Country harbours and are referred to in the text but not always shown on the harbour plans. Harbour dues are not listed as they are liable to alteration; for the same reason telephone numbers have been omitted except in a few cases where prior arrangements should be made for berthing. It is not possible within the compass of a pilot book of this size to give all the navigational information and other details available in the official publications, as for example local bye-laws. Such regulations exist in most commercial harbours. They may include speed limits, usually of 5 to 6 knots, and sometimes provide regulations additional to Rule 9(b) of the Collision Regulations '*that a vessel of less than 20 metres in length or a sailing vessel shall not impede the passage of a vessel which can safely navigate only within a narrow channel or fairway.*' This is only common sense, but it is important that visiting yachtsmen should know and obey the regulating signals which are included in this book for entry into commercial harbours.

It is emphasized again that the plans and text in this book are intended to be associated with up-to-date *Reed's Nautical Almanac* and coastal charts. They provide concise information for the main channels in the harbours but to obtain the maximum enjoyment from sailing and exploring the shallower channels and creeks of the big harbours, such as Chichester, Poole and Falmouth, a large-scale chart is desirable; hence the Admiralty chart number is added where appropriate after the plan number. Some of the Admiralty charts do not show the upper reaches of rivers, such as the Dart and Tamar which are navigable only near HW, and for these the 'Y' charts are recommended. They are published by Imray, Laurie, Norie & Wilson, Wych House, St Ives, Huntingdon, Cambridgeshire.

The preparation of this new edition has proved a difficult task owing to the numbers of changes in the details of the harbours notified while the work has been in progress. Time after time corrections, which in total number hundreds, have had to be made to the harbour plans and likewise much of the text has been altered and sometimes rewritten several times. Major corrections have come from *Notices to Mariners* but, as stated in *The Mariner's Handbook*, these do not include less important information which does not reach the Admiralty Chart until its next major correction. Thus, apart from my visiting the harbours west of Littlehampton by sea over the past few years, including twenty-five in 1975, most of the alterations are derived from local sources.

Great care has been taken in the compilation and revision of this book and nearly every chapter and harbour plan has been submitted for approval to the appropriate harbour authority or to an experienced local yachtsman. Nevertheless, there remains the possibility of undetected error such as inevitably may arise in individual work and, having pointed this out, no responsibility can be accepted for mistakes or omissions. Changes in sand formations and bars occur from time to time. Alterations in lights, beacons and buoys, traffic regulations, etc. are more frequent and for these the latest *Nautical Almanac* should always be consulted. This is particularly necessary in view of the forthcoming introduction of the IALA (International Association of Lighthouse Authorities) buoyage system. Diagrams illustrating the symbols and abbreviations of the IALA buoyage system 'A' are reproduced on the back end papers of this book. The reader is also referred to *Reed's Nautical Almanac* where the new system is fully explained and accompanied by illustrations in colour.

Finally, the author would like to add that he will be most grateful to receive corrections, constructive criticisms or additional information. Letters should be addressed to him c/o the publishers: Messrs Faber and Faber Ltd, 3 Queen Square, London, WC1N 3AU.

K.A.C.
April 1976

Times of High Water The average time differences for each harbour applied to the time of HW Dover have been supplied by the Institute of Oceanographic Sciences, or have been estimated where data are not available. To arrive at the time of HW in a harbour take the time of HW at Dover from *Reed's Nautical Almanac* or the *Yachting World Diary* and add or subtract the difference. These constants are only approximate where harbours are situated at a long distance from Dover; for greater accuracy refer to the predicted times of HW for the standard ports in ATT or the *Nautical Almanac* and for secondary ports apply the time differences which are also given.

Double High Waters occur at Southampton, in the West Solent ports and are even more evident at Christchurch and Poole. For these harbours the first HW at spring tides is included in the tidal data and in the Solent the second HW occurs about 2 hours later. HW at neap tides is always later than first HW springs, but there are long stands of tide, sometimes existing for several hours. Hence the average times of local HW referred to Dover would at best be poor approximations. However, predictions for each individual day of the year can be found in ATT and the *Nautical Almanac*.

Charted Depths and Data The charted depths given in this book indicate the depth of water *below chart datum* which is reduced to the level of LAT, or the drying heights (figures underlined) above it. Figures are given in the tidal data for each harbour for extra water at MHWS, MLWS, MHWN and MLWN which may be added to the charted depths or interpolated for intermediate states of tide. It will be noted that in many harbours om6 (2 ft) may be added to the charted depths at MLWS and as much as 1m8 (6 ft) at MLWN; these are of great significance when navigating in shallow channels. Also note that tidal levels are affected by meteorological conditions. For example, fresh northerly to easterly winds may bring low runs of tide sometimes lowering the levels to the extent of om6 (2 ft).

Distances at sea are expressed in nautical miles or on land in statute miles and kilometres.

Approach The directions assume that the vessel is approaching from seaward, and objects are described on the port or starboard hand of a ship entering the harbour.

Notation of Charts—Lights Lights outside harbours only are shown, except (1) leading lights placed inside, and (2) important buoys used for proceeding up harbour.

Lights are symbolized, the word 'light' or 'Lt' omitted.

Nature of light is noted, e.g. F, fixed, Gp Fl, group flashing, etc., and in the case of other than white lights, the colour, e.g. R, G, etc. followed by elevation in metres (m) and range (M) miles. Bearings are generally expressed to the nearest degree true and cardinal or half cardinal points are used only to indicate approximate directions. The limits of sectors and arcs of visibility and the alignment of directional lights and leading lights are given as *seen by an observer from seaward*. Lights are liable to alteration and in cases of doubt reference should always be made to the latest *Nautical Almanac*.

Buoys are symbolized, word 'buoy' omitted. Colour and shape are not always described, but symbol conforms to shape of buoy and, where scale allows, to configuration, i.e. solid black for black buoys, outline or patched shading for white or red, chequers and stripes shown as such. The positions of mooring buoys cannot always be shown on the harbour plans, often being precluded by scale, but visitors' moorings are referred to in the text.

Beacons are either symbolized or shown as small round 'o'. Point where pole crosses base line indicates exact position.

Coloured Area   Heavy stipple, indicates parts which dry out at LAT. Blue indicates parts where there are less than 2 metres at LAT and is bounded by dotted line. All over 2 metres are left white.

Anchorage Symbol (⚓) is intended to draw attention to proximity of anchorage, and does not necessarily indicate precise or only spot for letting go. Anchorages are being increasingly occupied by moorings, but are referred to in the text.

Minor posts, withys, dolphins, etc., inside harbours are sometimes precluded by scale.

ABBREVIATIONS TIDAL

ATT	Admiralty Tide Tables
HW	High Water
LW	Low Water
LAT	Lowest Astronomical Tide
MHHW	Mean Higher High Water
MHWS	Mean High Water Springs
MHWN	Mean High Water Neaps
MLWS	Mean Low Water Springs
MLWN	Mean Low Water Neaps

OTHER ABBREVIATIONS

Alt	Alternating
B	Black
Bl	Blue
BlW	Blue and White
Bn	Beacon
BW	Black and White
BY	Black and Yellow
Cheq	Chequers
Con	Conical
Dir	Directional
ev	Every
F	Fixed
Fl	Flashing
FS	Flagstaff
G	Green
Gp	Group
H	Horizontal
h.	hour(s)
HM	Harbour Master
Int Qk Fl	Interrupted quick flashing
Iso	Isophase
Km	Kilometres
LFl	Long flashing
Lt	Light
Lt Ho	Lighthouse
Lt V	Light-vessel
m	Metres
m.	minutes (time)
M	Miles (nautical) or land miles as appropriate
Mag	Magnetic
Mo	Morse Code Signal
Occ	Occulting
Occas	Occasional
Or	Orange
PA	Position approximate
Qk Fl	Quick flashing
R	Red

Ra Refl	Radar Reflector	V Qk Fl	Very quick flashing
Ro Bn	Radiobeacon	W	White
RW	Red and White	Y	Yellow
RY	Red and Yellow		
S	Stripes	CONVERSIONS	
sec.	seconds (time)	*Cable*	$\frac{1}{10}$ sea mile
Sph	Spherical	*International Nautical Mile*	1.85 km
Tr	Tower	*Statute Mile*	1.69 km
Vert	Vertical	*Fathom*	1.83 metres
vis	Visible		

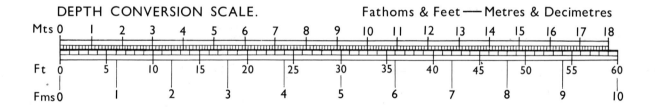

DEPTH CONVERSION SCALE.   Fathoms & Feet —— Metres & Decimetres

PART I

HARBOURS AND ANCHORAGES

RAMSGATE

Plan No. 1

High Water *+ 00h. 20m. Dover.*
Heights above Datum *MHWS 4m9. MLWS 0m4.*
MHWN 3m8. MLWN 1m2.
Depths *Off the entrance the depths are variable. Best water,*
usually about 1m4, lies on the west side of entrance deepening to
2m0 on this side between the pier ends. On the east side a bar often
forms which dries out at LAT. For depths within harbour see Plan
No. 1 and anchorage *below, but water is much influenced by wind*
direction. In the Inner Harbour depths are maintained at a fairly
constant level of 3m0.

RAMSGATE is the most easterly of the harbours south of the Thames. It is conveniently situated for yachts making passage from the English Channel to the North Sea or vice versa. The town is adjacent to the harbour and all facilities are available.

Approach and Entrance Approaching from the south either the Ramsgate Channel or the Gull Stream can be used. The Ramsgate Channel lies between Sandwich flats on the west and the Brake sand on the east. It is buoyed; after passing through the channel the North Fairway buoy (unlit) will be identified and left to port. Then steer for the entrance on a line from North Fairway buoy to a white diamond mark on the east pier below the watch-house. On the flood the tide sets strongly east across the entrance and allowance must be made to avoid being swept against the east pierhead or over the shoal lying off it.

From the eastward or northward from the Gull Stream use the Old Cudd Channel. This is entered by bringing the light pillar on the east pierhead in line with the lighthouse on the west pierhead at 291° 34′. This leaves the Quern red can buoy (at the north end of the Quern shoal) close to port and the unmarked spit (1m5) of the Dike sand close to starboard.

When about a cable from the east pierhead bear away to the south-west to give the shoals off the east pierhead a wide berth

1. *Ramsgate entrance approaching from south approx. on leading line 021°. This is the only correct angle of approach.*

and enter the harbour on the west side of the entrance. This will avoid the strong tidal set close to the east pier and also the shoal off it.

Note that the shoals outside the harbour are constantly shifting and the buoys and marks are moved from time to time.

Berthing directions are given from the watch-house on the east pier.

Tidal Signals   There are no tidal signals displayed in the daytime. At night the tidal light on west pier is F R when the depth is 3m0 or over; G when less than 3m0. During fog a bell at east pier ringing 10 strokes every quarter hour indicates 3m0 or over; 5 strokes slowly, less than 3m0.

Traffic Signals from east pier flagstaff: black flag indicates vessel(s) about to enter harbour and outward vessel(s) to keep clear. At night a white revolving light is exhibited. Two black balls (or red revolving light at night) indicate vessel(s) about to leave harbour; inward vessel(s) may not enter or approach harbour.

Lights   East pierhead Lt Occ W 10 sec. 8m 4M. This is also front light for the Old Cudd Channel, the rear light being west pier F R or G (see Tidal Signals), 4M, and these lights in line are 291° 34′. West pier is front Lt F R or G for south leading line and in line with F G Lt 4M high up on east cliff. These in line bear 020° 45′. *Fog Signal :* Bell from east pier.

If proceeding to the Inner Basin steer to pass between the two Qk Fl R Lts which are exhibited near HW time when the gates are open. Leave the two F R Vert Lts at the south-east corner of the west bank quay to port and two similar F R Vert Lts on the dolphin (see plan) to starboard.

Anchorage   Outside, south of harbour in Pegwell Bay under favourable conditions. No anchoring is permitted in the harbour as the central channel must be kept clear for larger vessels and the remainder is foul with moorings.

Visiting yachts are usually directed from the watch-house to

2.   Ramsgate entrance from south-east. It is from this angle of approach that a sailing yacht might risk being set on to the east pier.

3. Ramsgate, west pier and light. This is the correct side for entry. (Photo : Rozelle Raynes)

lie by the wall of the west pier in 1m7 or alongside the east pier in 2m0. The moorings in the south-west of the harbour are reserved for local yachts.

Inner Harbour The dock gates to the basin open about 2 hours before HW and close 1 hour after HW. Lights Qk Fl R on east and west sides of dock gates.

Traffic Signals Daytime: same as outer harbour. Night: two G Lts Vert on mast, vessels may enter. One R over two G Lts, vessels may leave. One R Lt only indicates dock gates will not open at all.

Berthing Directions These will be given by the Dock Master as the yacht enters. The level is maintained at about 3m0, but note that there is a three-year plan to turn the whole Inner Harbour into a marina for 482 boats and work is in progress on this. Note that part of the marina has since been opened.

Facilities Water at all piers on application. Petrol and oil, etc. available. Shops adjacent. EC Thurs. Boat-builders and repairers. Patent slip and scrubbing. Launching site slipways in outer harbour—see HM. Yacht club: R. Temple Y.C.

SANDWICH

High Water *at bar + ooh. 15m. Dover.*
Heights above Datum *Richborough : MHWS 3m7. MHWN 2m6. Bar dries at LW.*
Tides *The ebb runs for 7 hours and the flood for 5 hours at Sandwich Town, but the current continues upstream for a short while after HW and downstream for a short time after LW.*
Depths *On the bar dries om3 to om9 at chart datum. Entrance channel and river shallow. At HW Springs navigable with a maximum draught of about 4m5 or about 3mo at Neaps as far as Sandwich.*

SANDWICH, one of the Cinque Ports, lies 4½ miles from the mouth of the River Stour. It is a town of considerable historic interest. Visiting yachts lying by the town quay are within two minutes' walk of the town centre and there is a good hotel adjacent to the quay.

Approaches and Entrance The entrance to the River Stour lies at the south-west corner of Pegwell Bay, about ¾ mile south-west of Ramsgate, and the three huge cooling towers of the power station are very conspicuous from far out to sea. Pegwell Bay dries out except for a narrow channel carrying the river water. The channel across the bay is well marked with buoys, RW to port and B to starboard at the seaward end, and by posts with can-shaped topmarks to port and conical topmarks to starboard at the landward end. A small tower has been erected on the southern side of the channel, at the intersection of the posts and buoys with a Lt Fl R ev 10 sec. and a tide gauge. A further tower is planned for the north side of

4. *The power station and the dolphin near the mouth of River Stour. (Photo : Rozelle Raynes)*

the channel, opposite the first one; it is anticipated that this will also be lit. Eventually it is hoped that there will be a pair of leading lights for entering the river at night. The buoys and posts are subject to changes of position at short notice owing to the shifting sands.

The whole coastline near Shell Ness has advanced northward in a curved bulge, which has caused the whole channel to change its course. It is gradually getting nearer to the coast between Ramsgate and Sandwich. Approach only in good weather and *not* in a fresh easterly wind. From the lighthouse on the end of the west pier at Ramsgate steer 200° for a black conical buoy, B 3. From there the course is about 320° (but liable to change) to the buoyed entrance channel. Keep an eye open for hovercraft as their flight path (which is marked by orange spherical buoys) from the Hoverport at the north-west of Pegwell Bay converges at its seaward end with the course of a boat making for B 3 buoy from Ramsgate. The red can buoy almost due north of B 3 no longer exists.

Once inside the river keep to the middle. There is a dubious 4m5 MHWS and 3m0 MHWN as far as Sandwich, with hard bottom (thin layer of sludge over chalk). The swing bridge over the quay may be opened by giving 24 hours' notice; there is then 12 miles of navigable water for small yachts and boats up to 1m2 draught, and a Bailey bridge with about 3m6 clearance. The entrance channel and lower reaches are navigable from about $1\frac{1}{2}$ hours before until $2\frac{1}{2}$ hours after HW for a boat with 1m2 draught. Note that just inside the river on the starboard hand is a dolphin which is surmounted by a pole with diamond topmark.

Lights Do not attempt to enter at night or in fog without local knowledge until the proposed lights have been established.

Anchorage and Quay Anchor south-west of North Fairway buoy (unlit) in 1m5 clear of Hovercraft and wait for daylight, if conditions are favourable. Once inside the river there is a yacht marina about 1 mile below the town of Sandwich on the north bank. Here there is about 2m4 MHWS and 1m8 MHWN, but the berths dry at LW and hence are suitable only for yachts and boats which can take the bottom. The river becomes narrower and very congested in this reach owing to numerous moorings. Further downstream Richborough Wharf is private and is used by the tankers feeding the power station. There is another small commercial wharf a

5. *Sandwich—looking down river from the swing bridge. (Photo: Rozelle Raynes)*

short distance upstream belonging to Pfizer's. At Sandwich the bottom is hard chalk covered by a very thin layer of mud. For deep draught yachts it is wise to make preparations for drying out by the wall.

Facilities Sandwich Sailing and Motor Boat Club, boat-building yard and most facilities at marina. Water also at Sandwich Town Quay on application to tollbridge keeper. Petrol at garage near quay. Shops. EC Wed. Hotels. Yacht yard above bridge. Sandwich M.B. Club near marina have a slip.

DOVER

Plan No. 3

Heights above Datum *MHWS 6m9. MLWS 0m8. MHWN 5m3. MLWN 2m0 ; but irregular, depending on wind conditions.*

Depths *Dover is a large artificial harbour divided into two parts. The big expanse of the outer harbour is a deep-water port. The inner western part between the Admiralty pier and the Prince of Wales pier has about 5 m in the entrance, but the depths gradually reduce towards the inner tidal harbour, which dries out at LW except for a narrow channel 0m3 to 0m6 deep. Beyond this are the inner basins. The Wellington Dock, which is used by yachts, has 4m5 Springs, 3m3 Neaps. The Eastern Dock is deep.*

DOVER is a busy port on the south-east corner of England, but owing to its heavy commercial traffic yachtsmen are not encouraged to use the harbour unless they obey the traffic control signals implicitly. They are only welcome to stay for a maximum of two weeks in the Wellington Dock during the period 1st April–30th September.

Approach and Entrance Dover harbour is some 2 miles south-west of the South Foreland, and by day the long breakwaters make the harbour easy to identify and at night the breakwater lights will be seen at long range.

Yachts are encouraged to use the western entrance, whenever feasible, owing to the much heavier commercial traffic using the eastern one nowadays. *A careful look out should be kept for the entry signals*, and permission to enter should also be requested by Aldis lamp or International Code signals (SV I wish to enter; SW I wish to leave), or yachts fitted with VHF should call up Dover Port Control on Channel 12.

6. *Dover—panorama facing eastwards from cliffs.*

All yachts should keep well clear of the actual entrances until the moment they receive their entry or exit signals, in order to leave room for bigger ships to manœuvre or swing round just inside the entrances. This is easier at the eastern entrance as there is less tide and plenty of room between the Eastern Arm and the cliffs. Local tidal streams vary considerably and attain their maximum spring rate of 4 knots or more south of the Southern Breakwater. See Tidal Stream Diagrams, Admiralty Chart 1698.

Entrance Signals, Outer Harbour Western entrance, exhibited from gantry at signal station near seaward end of Admiralty pier.

By Day—Three red balls in triangle: vessels permitted to leave, no vessel is to enter or approach so as to obstruct the entrance. Two red balls vertical: vessels may enter with permission, no vessel to leave or approach so as to obstruct the entrance. Three red balls vertical: entrance is closed, for entering or leaving, for all traffic. These daytime signals are the same for both western and eastern entrances.

At Night—Subject to permission, etc. as by day. Three red lights in a triangle: vessels may leave harbour. Three white lights in a triangle: vessels may enter harbour. Three red lights vertical: entrance closed for entering or leaving.

Eastern entrance, exhibited from mast:

By Day—The same as for the western entrance.

At Night—One orange light at north end of Southern Breakwater and two green lights vertical at seaward end of Eastern Arm. These lights, *when shown seaward* and obscured towards the harbour, indicate that vessels may enter with permission, and unless these lights are being shown seaward no vessel is to enter or approach to obstruct the passage of any outward-bound vessel. These lights, *when shown towards the harbour and obscured seaward*, indicate that vessels are permitted to leave, and unless these lights are being shown

towards the harbour no vessel is to leave or approach to obstruct the passage of any inward-bound vessel. Three red lights vertical: entrance closed to all traffic entering or leaving (the same as for the western entrance).

Navigation in Outer Harbour The Harbour Patrol Launch will be found in the outer harbour. Yachts should beware of hovercraft channels across harbour, marked by a line of orange spherical buoys. They should also keep well clear of Channel ferries and cargo ships manœuvring in the fairway.

Inner Harbour When approaching the entrance to the basins in inner harbour avoid the Mole Head Rocks on north side of fairway extending south-eastwards from end of north pier. Anchorage is not permitted between Admiralty and Prince of Wales piers. The Granville Dock is not available to yachts. Permission should be asked of Dock Master to lie alongside cross wall until lock gates open when waiting to enter Wellington Dock.

Signals for tidal harbour and inner docks Red neon letters are displayed at height of 5m5, close to fixed green light at seaward end of Prince of Wales pier. They operate in conjunction with dock signals (for commercial vessels or very big yachts only). Small craft need not usually pay attention to these unless there is something big blocking the channel.

Fairway Signals by Day and Night—Letter 'W' Illuminated: Vessels are permitted to pass *inwards* through fairway from Outer Harbour to Tidal Harbour or Wellington Dock only, and no vessel may pass outwards whilst this signal is shown. Letter 'G' Illuminated: Vessels are permitted to pass *inwards* to Granville Dock, and no vessel may pass outwards, etc. No Signal Letter Illuminated: Vessels are permitted to pass *outwards* through fairway from Tidal Harbour to Outer Harbour, and *no vessel may pass inwards unless letters are illuminated.*

Wellington Dock Signals exhibited from top of 9m0 tower on

7. *Dover—outer harbour from Prince of Wales pier looking across yacht anchorage to castle.*

8. *Dover—looking into inner tidal harbour with Granville dock in background. Yachts pass up this harbour and turn to starboard at end for Wellington dock.*

9. *Dover—entrance to Wellington dock with gates open.*

west side of dock entrance. *By Day and Night*—Yellow Panel Illuminated (visible to seaward): Vessels are permitted to enter Wellington Dock, and none may leave dock or Tidal Harbour whilst this signal is shown. Red Panel Illuminated (visible to dock): Departure permitted from Wellington Dock and no vessel may enter dock or Tidal Harbour whilst this signal is shown.

Note: (a) At night a fixed all-round R Lt will be exhibited simultaneously on each of the north and south pierheads during tide times. (b) A single G Lt is displayed at cope level on each side of the Granville or Wellington Dock entrances when a vessel is about to enter or leave the dock.

Anchorage, etc. East of and protected from west by Prince of Wales pier, as near to the shore as soundings permit. The Royal Cinque Ports Y.C. has one visitors' mooring which may be used by yachts between April and September. Members have private moorings off the club but these may not be picked up without prior permission from the club. Yachts are not permitted to use the Camber or Eastern Docks. In bad weather pass into inner Wellington Dock, which is open from approx. 1 hour before HW until just after HW.

Lights At western entrance Lt Fl W 7½ sec. 21 m 20M is exhibited on the west side from a white tower on the end of the Admiralty pier. On the east side there is a Lt R Occ 30 sec. 21 m 18M at the south-west end of the Southern Breakwater, and at the knuckle a Lt Occ W seaward, R shoreward 10 sec. 15 m, 15–13M. At the eastern entrance there is an Or Lt traffic signal 4M at the northern end of the Southern Breakwater and traffic signals are exhibited at the south end of the Eastern Arm. Within the harbour there is a F G all-round Lt 4M at end of Prince of Wales pier, and there are lights at the Eastern Docks and elsewhere—see Plan No. 3 or Chart 1698.

Fog Signals Diaphone 10 sec. at end of Admiralty pier. Diaphone (2) ev 30 sec. at south end of Eastern Arm. Within the harbour, bell (2) 15 sec. at Prince of Wales pier. At the Eastern Dock siren (2) 10 sec. at Camber 'A' pier when required by ferries and siren 5 sec. at end of 'B' pier.

Facilities Water at Wellington Dock or by courtesy at yacht club. Chandlery, fuel and stores available. EC Wed. Scrubbing and minor repairs at Dolphin Hard by arrangement at Dock Master's office. Yacht club: R. Cinque Ports Y.C. Launching site: from beach below centre promenade, boats up to 4m8 long. Car park. Two stations. Buses to all parts.

FOLKESTONE

Plan No. 4

High Water — *00 h. 12 m. Dover.*
Heights above Datum *MHWS 7m1. MLWS 0m7.
MHWN 5m7. MLWN 2m0.*
Depths *The outer harbour is dredged to a least depth of 4m5 and is formed by the breakwater which extends into deep water. In the entrance to the inner harbour there is 5m5 at MHWS and from 3m3 to 4m2 MHWS within the harbour, and at Neaps 1m0 less. At LW it dries out.*

FOLKESTONE has a heavy commercial traffic owing to the roll-on roll-off ferry terminal with eight services a day. The inner harbour is only suitable for yachts with legs or those prepared to dry out by the rough wall at the east pier. It is not a good refuge in bad weather and yachts are only welcome for occasional overnight mooring as the whole inner harbour is full up. The inner harbour faces east but the entrance itself receives extra protection from the west by a long breakwater built for the British Rail steamers and which forms the outer harbour. The inner harbour is mostly used by fishing boats equipped with legs. The town itself has all the facilities of a summer holiday resort.

Approach and Entrance Folkestone is about 5½ miles westward of Dover and is the largest town situated on the coast between Dungeness and the Foreland. The town is thus easy to recognize and the harbour lies nearer its eastern end, behind a conspicuous outer breakwater. There are rocky ledges to the west of the breakwater and east of the inner harbour entrance. Of these the Mole Head Rocks, less than 2 cables east of the

inner end of the outer breakwater, and the ledges off Copt Point are the more dangerous. To clear these when approaching from the east keep the South Foreland well open of the Dover cliffs. By night, the South Foreland light is masked northward of 58° true, so that the vessel should not go northward of the arc of the light. Eddy on east stream. Then when the south end of the east pier (Qk Fl W) of the inner harbour bears 305° alter course leaving the outer breakwater to port. Sufficient rise of tide is required as the water shoals about 2 cables off the inner harbour and shelves gradually to — 1m0 at the entrance. For depths within the harbour see *Anchorage and Harbour.*

Signals at the outer end of the new ferry pier are shown for car ferries by means of a black flag or 1, 2 or 3 spherical shapes.

Lights, etc. Outer breakwater Gp Fl W (2) 10 sec. 14m 22M. Occasional leading lights F R and F G exhibited at the knuckle of outer breakwater and on or near the ferry pier when a car ferry is expected. East pierhead Qk Fl W Occas. Two F R on mole at south quay when commercial vessel about to enter. Fog diaphone (4) 60 sec. at breakwater head continuously if visibility is less than 1M.

Anchorage and Harbour (1) Anchorage outside the inner harbour is inadvisable owing to the ferry traffic and risk of fouling the ground moorings and long chains used for winching off the ferries. It is also exposed and has indifferent holding ground. No yacht may *ever* moor alongside the ferry pier except in dire medical emergency. (2) Yachts may lie in the inner harbour if there is room inside the east pier on legs or alongside the pier. At LAT the harbour dries 1m0 at the entrance, about 2m2 in the centre and up to 3m7 at the northern end of the east pier. Yachtsmen must calculate the tide level by reference to the heights above datum at the head of the chapter, but it is said that boats up to 1m5 draught can enter 3 hours either side of HW. The swing bridge at western

10. Folkestone. Inner harbour looking across entrance which is on right. Firm clean bottom to dry on legs or lie by east wall.

end of inner harbour is permanently fixed and the shallow inner basin (controlled by Folkestone Corporation) can be entered only by boats able to pass below it.

Facilities Water at quay. Good shopping centre, EC Wed. Station. Buses to all parts. Yacht club: Folkestone S.C. near slipway in inner harbour.

RYE

Plan No. 5

High Water *at entrance* −00 h. 05 m. *Dover.*
Heights above Datum *near approach* : *MHWS 7m7.
MHWN 6m0. Dries LW. Harbour MHWS 5m3. MHWN 3m6.*
Depths *In the channel there is only a fresh-water trickle at
MLWS. At MHWS there is about 3m4 to 4m5 in the harbour
alongside the catwalk staging and 1m6 to 2m8 at MHWN.*

11. *The entrance to Rye, view from the south-east (at LW).*

RYE HARBOUR is ¾ mile within the entrance, and is a small
village. The town itself is another 2 miles up the river, which is
navigable at high water and is increasingly used by cargo
vessels; it is one of the Cinque Ports and so charming that it
attracts many visitors. There are good hotels.

Rye harbour entrance once had a somewhat bad reputation
owing to the loss of the lifeboat crew west of the entrance in
1928. Since then, however, the entrance has been improved
and it is clearly marked. Given an offshore wind and fair
weather and the right state of tide, strangers should not find
the entrance unduly difficult. A south-west wind Force 5 is
definitely uncomfortable and probably too much for a first
attempt. Power is desirable, as the tide runs very hard in the
narrow channel—the flood is stronger than the ebb, which is
unusual in rivers.

Approach and Entrance The entrance lies at the apex of
Rye Bay. From the eastward follow the low coast from
Dungeness for some 7 miles keeping about a mile offshore until
the Rye Fairway buoy and the conspicuous west pier and the
tripod beacon are seen. Westward of the entrance the shore is
also low (but hills behind) for a distance of 5 miles to Fairlight,
which is high and can be recognized by the square tower of the
church, and its coastguard station.

The entrance and channel to Rye harbour, from 30 to 45m
wide, lie between the east and west piers, and on the west side
is a long training wall which extends to seaward of the entrance.
This training wall is covered between half tide and HW
(depths above 2m4), and it is marked by a series of pole
beacons with cage topmarks some on top of dolphins, and three
Qk Fl R Lts at night placed at irregular intervals along the wall
as far as the Harbour Office and three Fl R Lts at the bend
beyond it. At its seaward extremity there stands a tripod light
dolphin Fl R 5 sec. 7m 6M. The east pier is also long, though it
does not extend as far seaward, and at the end of it there is a
light post Fl W 2½ sec. 7m 4M. At MHWS the tops of this east
pier are just showing, but it is marked by two posts with conical
topmarks.

12. The entrance and east pier near HW from the root of the west pier. The port hand cages mark the submerged training wall.

The RW Sph Rye Fairway buoy (Qk Fl W) is placed 1.85 miles from the harbour entrance. Vessels making for Rye should head up towards this buoy, then alter course to 329° to enter the harbour. There is always an easterly set across the harbour entrance, especially on the flood tide. Within the entrance a course mid-channel is possibly the best to take, although the deeper water is on the west side. However, care must be taken on the flood when side currents flowing across the training wall may affect steering. The cage beacons are fixed to the *inside* edge of the training wall except for one off the HM's office.

The entrance should not be approached by vessels with a draught of 2m earlier than 3 hours before HW, and the best time to enter is from 1 hour before HW; the best time to leave is not later than 1 hour after HW (but for yachts of moderate draught 2½ hours either side is possible with care at Springs). A tide gauge is fitted to the end of the eastern breakwater.

Tidal Signals are shown by day from a mast just behind the Harbour Office, about ¾ mile within the entrance on the east side, and by night from the roof of the Office when any merchant ship (irrespective of size) is expected, but the signals are hard to see in poor visibility. *By day :* 2m4 on bar, one ball on yard; 2m9 on bar, one ball on each yard; 3m0 on bar, one ball at masthead only; 3m3 on bar, one ball at masthead, one ball on yard; 3m6 on bar, one ball at masthead, one ball on each yard. *By night :* 2m4 to 3m0, a green light; over 3m0, a red light.

Traffic Signals When a cargo vessel is moving in the harbour a black ball is hoisted by day or an amber Qk Fl Lt is exhibited on Harbour Office at night; all vessels must give way.

Lights, etc. From beacon on western arm extension Fl R

31

13. Looking up river from the slip at Rye harbour (near HW). Yachts on right are at the catwalk staging.

5 sec. 7m 6M; on eastern pier end Fl W 2½ sec. 7m 4M. Lights on east side of channel leading up the channel at 329°: front, Qk Fl G; rear, Occ W G with W sector 326.5° − 331.5°. Qk Fl R on beacons or dolphins on west side of channel as previously referred to. Fog diaphone on western arm extension.

Anchorage and Berths In fair weather yachts awaiting the tide for Rye should anchor close to Rye Fairway buoy (where there is a least depth of 5m9). In west or south-west winds yachts should anchor behind Dungeness, close to the Coastguard's House. With sufficient rise of tide all visiting

14. Looking downstream at LWS, catwalk staging on left. Harbour Master's house centre.

yachts should moor at special berths provided alongside the stagings at Rye harbour village, about a mile from the entrance on the east side of the river, just beyond the HM's Office. This is about 2 miles from Rye town. The berths are lighted at night. Double mooring is not allowed. Care should be taken when turning at Rye harbour village at springs.

The large range of tide calls for careful mooring, as winds blowing on to the staging have been the cause of many broken masts or damaged spreaders. Yachts will lie afloat for about 4 hours, then take the bottom, which is hard muddy shingle. A vacant berth may indicate wreckage below water—always consult the HM.

Facilities Water is available from a hose-pipe at the south end of catwalk staging—apply to HM (Tel. Camber 225). Petrol and oil at Strand quay. Hose-pipe at corner of catwalk above visitor's berth. Stores at Rye town 2 miles away, (3.2 km) or limited supply in Rye harbour or at caravan site to south of village by the Martello tower. EC Tues. PO at harbour and town. Small boat-builders. Launching site: slip with road access at Rye harbour village, but is only usable for a few hours either side of HW (a power cable marked by beacons runs across near here to the lighthouse). Yacht club: Rye Harbour S.C. opposite Harbour Office. Station at Rye town. Bus service from harbour to town, whence buses to all parts.

NEWHAVEN

Plan No. 6

High Water *− 00 h. 13 m. Dover.*
Heights above Datum *MHWS 6m6. MLWS 0m6.*
MHWN 5m2. MLWN 1m9.
Depths *Dredged to 5m5 in the entrance, to 3m0 along East*
Wharf to Sleeper's Hole, 2m4 up to west side Ballast Wharf and
not less than 1m2 to bridge. Silting and dredging continually
occurring.

NEWHAVEN is primarily a commercial port but it also offers
good facilities for yachts in the marina. The town itself is not
interesting, but the distance by bus to Seaford or Eastbourne is
short, and there are pleasant walks if weather-bound.

There is a regular steamer service to Dieppe and the harbour
is used by other commercial vessels. The cross-Channel boats
on occasion warp off by means of a steel hawser run across the
harbour and incoming ones may swing outside the harbour to
enter stern first.

Approach and Entrance Newhaven harbour lies just
over 7 miles west of Beachy Head, and 3 miles west of Seaford
Head. The town of Seaford is 5 miles westward of Beachy
Head and for some 2 miles west of Seaford the shore is low and
shingly. At the western end of Seaford Bay is Burrow Head,
and just eastward at the foot of this is Newhaven. The big
breakwater at the entrance is conspicuous and makes an easily
recognizable landmark.

From the eastward stand well away from Seaford Head and
steer for position off Burrow Head. Alter course when the
entrance bears north, and leave to the westward the outer
breakwater, steering in toward the east pier, which is some 3
cables away. In bad weather, with an onshore wind, there is an
awkward sea off the entrance southward of the breakwater.
Steer up mid-channel observing signals shown at southern end

15.   Newhaven breakwater and view across bay to Seaford Head.

34

16. *Newhaven harbour, showing marina on west side.*

of west pier. Within $\frac{1}{2}$ mile of shore, the west-going stream starts about $1\frac{1}{2}$ to 2 hours before HW.

Signals   By day signals consist of red fluorescent spherical shapes (or balls) displayed from mast at base of lighthouse on west pier. One ball indicates a vessel may enter but not leave. Two balls vertical that a vessel may not enter but may leave. Three black balls, port temporarily closed to all traffic. Between sunrise and sunset craft of 10m7 or less in length may (at the time of writing) enter or leave the harbour without any prescribed signal being exhibited. By night from lighthouse: G all-round Lt indicates that a vessel may enter but not leave. R Lt, may leave but not enter. Three R Vert, port temporarily closed.

Lights, etc.   At end of outer (western) breakwater Lt Gp Occ (2) W 10 sec. 17m 12M; at end of east pier, Iso G Lt 5 sec. 12m 6M. Small F R Lt on west pier and F G on east pier, a cable inside entrance. Diaphone outer breakwater head ev 30 sec. Tide-gauge near base of lighthouse on west pier. When entering at night keep R Lt on Packet Wharf open between F R and F G Lts on west and east piers.

Anchorage and Berths   (1) Outside off Seaford in settled weather, dangerous if wind shifts onshore. (2) All yachts should seek instructions from Harbour Watch-house on west side of harbour. Space is limited but limited duration mooring sometimes available at berths on east side of harbour, with 2mo. (3) Some berthing facilities available in marina in Sleeper's Hole, 3 cables within entrance on porthand side. Marina watch-house at head of southern marina jetty. Additional moorings in U basin just northward.

Facilities   Fuel and water from marina fuelling pontoon. Ship chandlers, and all stores obtainable. EC Wed. Yacht yard, yacht marina, gridirons and scrubbing hard. Launching site at Sleeper's Hole on application at Cresta Marine. Yacht club: Newhaven & Seaford S.C. Station and numerous buses to all parts.

SHOREHAM

Plan No. 8

High Water — *00 h. 03 m. Dover.*
Heights above Datum *at entrance MHWS 6m2. MLWS
0m7. MHWN 5m0. MLWN 1m9.*
Depths *The lowest charted depth in the approach is 1m7
LAT and 2m1 in the entrance. The dredged depths within the
harbour are shown on Plan No. 8, but these are liable to silting and
only hold good immediately after dredging.*

SHOREHAM HARBOUR consists of a western arm which is the
mouth of the River Adur, and a short eastern arm leading
through lock gates to the Southwick Canal.

Superficially Shoreham is a good yachting harbour, as once
through the locks into Southwick canal there are complete
shelter and good facilities, besides being in easy reach of
London. However, Shoreham is increasingly a very busy
commercial port with little room left for casual private vessels,
so it is imperative that prior berthing arrangements are made.
Port bye-laws are obtainable from the HM. Arrival should be
reported within 24 hours and there are strict speed limits and
other regulations.

Approach and Entrance Shoreham harbour entrance is
about 4 miles west of Brighton Palace Pier. The most
conspicuous landmarks are the twin chimneys (marked at
night by red lights) of the power station about ¾ mile east-
north-east of the entrance, and another pair about 3¾ cables
beyond them. The entrance itself lies between two conspicuous concrete breakwaters. A Con BY Vert S buoy (Qk Fl)
nearly 3 cables east-south-east of the entrance marks the outer
end of a sewer outfall.

The shallowing water in the approach off the entrance can be
very rough in strong winds if at all onshore, particularly on the
ebb tide. Newhaven is a better port of refuge.

The leading lights consist of a low light on the duty officer's
cabin on the middle pier extremity and a high light at rear from
a grey circular tower. The structures are conspicuous leading
marks by day and approach to the harbour is best made on
their transit at 355°.

The entrance lies between the two concrete breakwaters and
within are east and west piers. Farther north there is a third
pier (the middle pier) on the fork of the western and eastern
arms.

Off the entrance the west-going stream starts about 2 hours
before HW and the east-going 6 hours later. During the west-
going stream there is a south-west set across the entrance from
the east breakwater towards the west breakwater, where part of
it is deflected into the entrance and then north-east towards the
end of the east pier. The eddy is strongest 1 hour before HW to
ebb 1 hour after HW.

The maximum rate of the main stream at the harbour
entrance is about 3 knots, but the flood sets into the western
arm, where it can attain 4 knots, and the ebb 5 knots in some
parts at springs. In the eastern arm there is practically no
stream, but a yacht should be piloted with caution in the
vicinity of the division off the middle pier.

The channel in the eastern arm is dredged and leads to the
locks into the Southwick canal. The western arm is only
suitable for visiting yachts if able to take the ground. Traffic
signals, given below, *must* be observed.

Controlling Signals *Middle Pier Control Station—*
Amber Lt Occ 3 sec. (day and night): no vessel shall enter the
Port for the purpose of proceeding to the eastern or western
arm and no vessel outside the Port entrance shall be navigated
in such a way as to hinder the passage of vessels leaving the

17. Just inside entrance showing west, middle and east piers. Also watch-house from where instructions are given, and signal flag-staff. High lighthouse to left, low light on watch-house to right at flagstaff.

Port. *Lifeboat House focusing over Eastern Arm*—R Lt Occ 3 sec. (day and night): no vessel shall proceed along the eastern arm for the purpose of leaving the Port, moving to another berth in the eastern arm or passing into the western arm of the Port. *Lifeboat House focusing over Western Arm*—R Lt Occ 3 sec. (day and night): no vessel shall proceed along the western arm for the purpose of leaving the Port, moving to another berth in the western arm or passing into the eastern arm of the Port.

Signals at Locks No vessel may approach to enter the canal until a green pennant by day or a green light by night is exhibited at the outer end of the lock. Similarly no vessel may approach to leave until a yellow pennant by day or an amber light by night is exhibited near the inner end of the lock. If a black ball by day or a red light at night is exhibited no vessel may approach for the purpose of entering the lock or mooring at the lead-in. During non-tidal periods instructions must be taken from the duty officer on the middle pier, who will give permission for yachts to anchor close to the eastward side of the middle pier.

Tidal Signals Low light (middle pier) shows red when the tide level does not exceed 2m47 above chart datum; green when 2m47–3m69 of water above chart datum; white when more than 3m69 above chart datum.

Lights, etc. East breakwater Lt Fl G 5 sec. 7m 4M. West breakwater Lt Fl R 5 sec. 7m 4M. These breakwater lights are

18. *Shoreham. The middle pier, showing in detail the watch-house with low light and Nauto on it. High lighthouse to right and rear.*

not always easy to pick up against the background of bright lights. Leading lights (in transit 355° true). High Lt (rear) Fl W 10 sec. 13m 15M. Low Lt (front) F W R or G 8m. 10, 9, 9M. (See **Tidal Signals** for change of colour.) *Fog Signals.* East breakwater: siren ev 2m. Middle pier: horn ev 20 sec. The latter is only sounded when ships are approaching.

Anchorages, etc. (1) Outside clear of fairway with offshore winds and settled weather in suitable depth of water, bottom mostly sand over clay or chalk. (2) Directions for berthing inside the harbour may be obtained from the duty officer on the middle pier at all times, but the Harbour Authority is virtually without facilities of its own for the berthing of yachts. As stated, prior berthing arrangements must be made with the local yards or clubs for berthing. *Western arm :* James Taylor, Watercraft, Sussex Motor Y.C., Lighthouse Club. *Eastern arm :* Truslers. *Southwick Canal :* Riverside Yard, Lady Bee, Sussex Yacht Club.

Facilities   Water at yards or by courtesy at Sussex Yacht Club. Petrol and oil at local garage adjacent to Southwick canal moorings as also yacht club, yards, gridiron and scrubbing. Launching sites from beach, adjacent to high lighthouse and middle pier, and from muddy public hards throughout the harbour. Yacht clubs: The Sussex Y.C., Sussex Motor Y.C., Lighthouse Club. Trains and frequent buses to Brighton and elsewhere.

BRIGHTON MARINA

THE IMPRESSIVE artificial yacht harbour at Brighton, which has been built seaward into the English Channel, is the most important marina development in this country. It provides berths for over 2,000 boats and is the principal yacht harbour between Ramsgate and Chichester. The marina will be opened while this book is in press, and hence only the provisional arrangements and plan can be given here in anticipation of the developments which will be completed (as soon as possible) in stages as required.

Approach and Entrance   The position of the marina is just over a mile east of Brighton Palace Pier. It consists of a long east breakwater and a west breakwater which extends farther seaward to protect the entrance from west to south-south-west, so that final approach should be made from a south-east direction. In strong winds or gales from this direction the approach would be very rough, but the harbour itself will be safe under all conditions. The spending beach and wave screen are designed to prevent any significant swell entering the inner harbour.

Lights etc.   At the end of the western breakwater head there is a light structure Qk Fl R 9½m 7M and at the head of the eastern breakwater north of it is the principal lighthouse Gp Fl (4) W R 20 sec. 16m 18M Red sector 260° to 295°; white 295° through north to 100°, obscured elsewhere. Fog diaphone (2) ev 30 sec. Here the plan also includes a radio beacon, callsign BT on same frequency as Chichester beacon (303.4 kHz) CH, both range 10M. A black conical fairway buoy Gp Fl (3) W 10 sec. 6M will be added in 1977 at a distance of 1 mile south-south-east of the harbour entrance, which will also serve as an offshore racing turning mark.

The least depth in entrance of main channel 3m0. Harbour Control is on port hand of the inner entrance.

Harbour and Facilities   The general layout is shown in the accompanying plan. The tidal basin has floating platforms and pontoon berths for boats up to 30m alongside with draughts ranging from 3m0 at the southern end to 1m5 at the northern. The fuelling pontoon is at its north-east end close to the locks to the locked basin and to the boatyard site and Travelift dock. In the locked basin there are 850 berths for boats up to 18m alongside and 2m4 draught. Between the tidal basin and the locked basin lie the extensive car parks. In Brighton there are all the facilities of a very large seaside town, including frequent express (under an hour) trains to London.

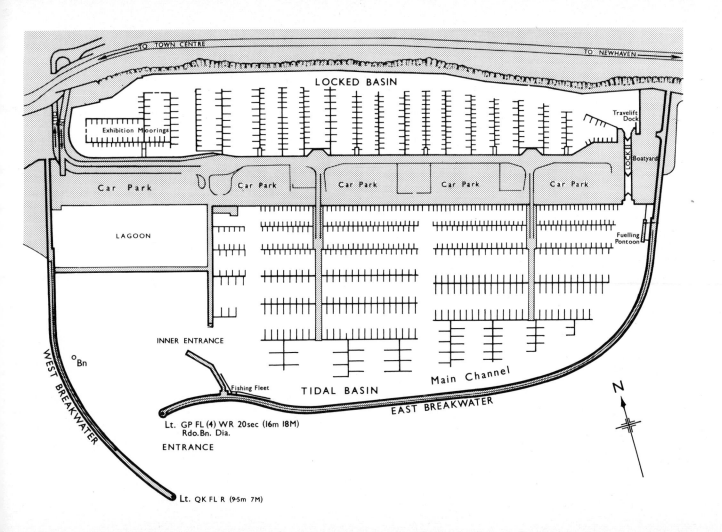

LITTLEHAMPTON

Plan No. 7

High Water *at entrance* +00 h. 04 m. Dover.
Heights above Datum *MHWS* 5m7. *MLWS* 0m5.
MHWN 4m6. *MLWN* 1m7.
Depths *About 0m2 on bar, deepening between the piers to about 1m2 to 2m4, which depths are maintained almost as far as the swingbridge.*

LITTLEHAMPTON is a convenient harbour for yachts except for the bar (0m2 but subject to change) which can only be crossed with sufficient rise of tide. Allowance has to be made for the strong streams in the entrance, and it is dangerous to approach in strong onshore winds. There are commercial shipping in the harbour and good facilities for yachts, with the town close by. Unfortunately there is the shortage of moorings referred to below. Half a mile above the swingbridge a new bridge has been built which has about 3m6 headroom at MHWS, and the fixed railway bridge at Ford has a clearance of 3m3 at HW. At Arundel a new road bridge has been built ¼ mile downstream of the old bridge with a clearance of 3m0 at MHWS. Craft which can pass under the bridges can navigate as far as Arundel, with a least depth of 1m3 MLWS the whole way.

Approach and Entrance The harbour is situated 10 miles east of Selsey Bill. The entrance lies between two piers easily recognizable from seaward and 2¼ miles south-west is the Winter Knoll red can buoy Fl (4) 15 sec. The western pier is the longer, and at its seaward end is a red barrel beacon. The eastern pier stops short at the esplanade, but there is a low dickerwork continuation built in the sands for about ¼ mile seawards. This is submerged from half tide to HW, but is

19.   Littlehampton looking into entrance from south on leading line.

20. *Littlehampton entrance showing starboard hand beacon and starboard hand posts marking underwater dickerwork. Main breakwater on left of picture.*

21. *Littlehampton. The lighthouse and funfair are conspicuous from seaward.*

marked by perches with small top crosses and at its extremity by a white luminous beacon. The leading marks for the entrance are the lighthouse at the inshore end of the short east breakwater and the black steel column for the light at the outer end in transit at 345°. The iron column may be visible only when in line and against the white background of the lighthouse. Keep nearer the eastern side when entering, if the tide is setting on to the western pier. The tide is very fierce up the

22. *Littlehampton harbour. Harbour office to left of chimney. Visiting yachts anchor opposite office and await berthing instructions.*

narrow harbour entrance. It turns to west along the shore nearly 2 hours before HW. Approach should not be attempted in strong onshore winds and on the ebb tide the entrance can be very rough. Newhaven is a better port of refuge.

Signals   When black-hulled pilot boat with large white 'P' at bow flies a R W flag by day or shows W over R Lts by night, all boats keep clear as a ship is about to enter or leave harbour. If ship signals one long and two short blasts, keep clear, particularly of narrows at entrance.

Lights   East pier front F R 6m 7M. Rear Occ W Or 7½ sec. 9m 10M. White 287° to 000°; orange then to 042°. Lts in line 345°. West pier unwatched FW 5m 6M.

Anchorage   (1) Outside, south of entrance at distance according to vessel's draught: This is slightly sheltered from the west by Selsey Bill and the Owers but is completely open from the south-west, through south to east-north-east. (2) In the past it has often been possible to obtain the temporary use of a mooring on application to the HM. At the present time however, the marina above the bridge is usually fully booked and the demand for permanent moorings is so great that in order to conserve safe navigation the HM has to warn visitors that they must stay with their boats in order that they may be moved should the need arise at short notice. Intending visitors should telephone the HM, Littlehampton 21215/16, to ascertain the latest mooring situation and avoid misunderstanding if it is impossible to offer facilities for a short stay.

Facilities   Water at HM's, or from yards. Petrol and oil. All stores. EC Wed. Several yacht yards. Launching sites: light boats from hard sand foreshore on west side down river of the Arun Y.C. Yacht clubs: Arun Y.C., Littlehampton S. & M.B. Station. Good service of buses.

CHICHESTER HARBOUR

Plan Nos. 9a and 9b. Admiralty Chart No. 3418

High Water *at entrance +00 h. 11 m. Dover.*
Heights above Datum *MHWS 4m9. MLWS 0m7. MHWN 4m0. MLWN 1m8.*
Depths *The water shoals nearly a mile south of the Chichester Bar beacon. On the correct approach least water on the bar is 0m7, but may vary from time to time. The entrance is deep and (except for a small shoal (1m5) north-north-east of North Winner buoy) there is ample water inside the harbour in the main channels and 2m4 off Itchenor.*

CHICHESTER HARBOUR is an ideal small boat centre. There is racing for all small classes and there are more sailing clubs than in any other harbour on the South Coast. The harbour is an interesting one with many channels to explore, and variety from the mud-banked creeks to the clean, sandy shores at the entrance. Bosham and Itchenor are both attractive villages, and altogether the harbour, though crowded, is well worth visiting. There is a speed limit of 8 knots within the harbour, and water skiing is prohibited.

The whole harbour including the Emsworth Channel is controlled by the Chichester Harbour Conservancy with the Manager/Harbour Master and his deputy centred at Itchenor Harbour Office. Many improvements have been completed but as the radical alterations include the new approach across the bar (at the West Pole beacon; to be renamed Chichester Bar beacon) and other new beacons and lights, it has been necessary to look ahead and incorporate proposals which will almost certainly be approved while this edition is at press.

These do not however include the changes anticipated on the introduction of the IALA lights and buoyage system which are referred to on the back end papers.

Approach and Entrance The entrance to Chichester harbour lies some 8 miles west of Selsey Bill. There are extensive sands extending seawards on both sides of the approach and entrance, named the West Pole, the Middle Pole and the East Pole. With strong onshore winds there can be a very ugly sea on the bar, especially on the ebb when the approach can be dangerous.

When approaching from east or west keep well offshore until one or both of the conspicuous marks have been identified. The Nab Tower bearing 184° or Chichester Bar beacon (Fl W R 5 sec.) bearing 004°. (Trial radio beacon callsign CH. (303.4 kHz) range 10M.) Then alter course for the beacon, which should be left about ½ cable on the port hand. In the approach the water shoals rapidly from 1 mile south of the beacon gradually falling to 0m7 at the beacon, where there is a tide-gauge which gives the level at chart datum. If the approach is made in thick weather the principal dangers are the East Pole sands, which extend over a mile south-east of the beacon, especially so when the stream is setting eastward, although its rate is moderate.

When Chichester Bar beacon is abeam the entrance to Chichester harbour lies immediately east of Eastoke Point, which is a sandy headland backed by trees and the end of the bungalow building, formerly Treloar Hospital. The distance from ½ cable east of the Chichester Bar beacon to the entrance is about a mile making good a course of 013° on the West Winner beacon (Fl W 5 sec.). This course carries 0m7 and lies between the West Pole and the Middle Pole sands. As Eastoke Point is approached the water becomes much deeper. Eastoke beacon (Qk Fl R) and small unlit beacons at the ends of groynes will be left to port and course may soon be altered to

23. *Chichester Bar Beacon with tide gauge. Leaving this about ½ cable to port steer for the entrance to the right of the clump of trees.*

follow up the entrance channel between the steep shingle shore on the port hand and the wide expanse of the Winner sands on the starboard hand. These dry at LW and are marked by the West Winner beacon (Fl 5 secs.) and the North-west Winner buoy (Gp Fl (3) W 10 sec.). In the entrance channel the tidal streams are fierce and may attain 2.8 knots on the flood or 6.4 knots on a big spring ebb about 2 hours after HW.

Within the entrance the channel divides into two arms. One leads in a northerly direction to Emsworth and is entered between Sandy Point and the Fishery buoy. It is wide and deep nearly as far as the junction with Sweare Deep, where there is a beacon Gp Fl (2) R 15 sec. Beyond this the channel is shallow and dried out at LW about ½ mile below the town. The other

arm bears round the north side of the Winner to the eastward and leads via the Chichester Channel to Itchenor, the Bosham Channel and to Dell Quay.

To enter the Chichester Channel (after passing Hayling Island Sailing Club and Sandy Point on the west side) bear to starboard to the eastward to leave to starboard the North-west Winner (Gp Fl (3) W 10 sec.), the North Winner (Fl W 10 sec.), the Mid Winner (Gp Fl (3) W 10 sec.) conical black buoys and the East Head beacon (Fl W 10 sec.) with tide-gauge. There is a shoal patch 1m5 close north-north-east of the North Winner buoy but otherwise the channel is from 2m4 to 7m deep. Leave to port following red can buoys: Stocker (Gp Fl (4) R 10 sec.), Copyhold (unlit) and Sandhead (Fl R 10 sec.).

24. Hayling Island S.C. and Sandy Point at end of the entrance on the west side.

The next pair of buoys are the North-east Sandhead (Gp Fl (2) R 10 sec.) to port and the Rookwood buoy to starboard. East of the North-east Sandhead buoy the channel bears to the North-east, where identify and bring 'Roman Transit beacon' (port hand daymark) main channel beacon (white rectangular daymark) on the shore in transit at 032° with Stoke Clump, a conspicuous clump of trees on the distant downs. If it is too misty to see these landmarks it does not matter, for the channel is clearly marked on the port hand by the Camber beacon (Qk Fl R) at the entrance of the Thorney Channel and on the starboard hand by the Chalkdock beacon (Fl 10 sec.) and by occasional perches, though these are situated high up on the mud and should be given a wide berth.

After passing the Chalkdock beacon alter course to round the black conical starboard hand Wear buoy (Gp Fl (3) 10 sec.) and then, on an approximately east Mag course, proceed up the next reach to the junction of the Bosham and Chichester Channels. The former buoy moored at the entrance to Bosham

Lake has been replaced by a junction beacon which is a starboard hand mark for the Bosham Channel and a port hand one for the Itchenor Reach with the Fairway Con B buoy (Fl W 10 sec.) to starboard. This channel is deep almost as far as Longmore Point about a mile east of Itchenor, where it then shallows but is marked by buoys.

The Bosham Channel carries 1m8 to within a cable or two of the village and is marked by perches.

The Thorney Channel is entered by leaving the Camber beacon (Qk Fl R) to starboard, and then leaving Pilsey Island and beacon (Fl R 10 sec.) to port and a black perch to starboard; neither should be passed close to. Then pass between a pair of beacons beyond which the channel is straight and marked by occasional perches. Depths range from 3m7 down to 1m8 to north-east of Stanbury Point.

Lights Chichester Bar beacon carries at Lt Fl W R 5 sec. 8M. showing W from 322° to 080° and R elsewhere. Approach in the white sector and leave the beacon ½ cable to port. Then

25. *East Head Beacon and East Head Sands.*

26. *Itchenor with Harbour Master's launch in foreground and office in the white building in line with her mooring buoy. The landing pontoon is to the right.*

27. Bosham Creek and church.

steer 013° for the West Winner beacon (Fl W 5 sec.) and after passing the Eastoke beacon port hand light (Qk Fl R) alter course up the entrance channel and proceed referring to the lights already stated in the text and shown in the harbour plans.

Anchorages and Berthing (1) In westerly winds just within the entrance north of Sandy Point outside local moorings. (2) Off East Head, beyond the beacon. Pleasant anchorage on sandy bottom in settled weather, but rather exposed except from south and east. A shallow creek marked by perches leads to the Roman Landing and West Wittering S.C. (3) In Chichester Channel south of the line of the Wear and Fairway buoys. (4) At Itchenor visiting yachts up to 10 tons should moor temporarily at the visitor's buoy (white with red band) opposite the HM's office. The HM or his deputy will then allocate a vacant mooring of which some are usually available. (5) In the Birdham Yacht Basin or the Chichester Yacht Basin. Allow for sufficient rise of tide as the main channel dries out near the Spit buoy. To reach the former leave the buoy to port and the BW perches leading to the lock close to starboard. To reach the Chichester Yacht Basin leave the buoy to starboard and continue up channel for 2 cables until two beacons on the mud to port come into line, then follow their transit to the six BW beacons which lead to the lock and should be left close to starboard. Yacht yard, fuel, water, stores, etc. at both marinas. (6) Bosham Lake. The historic village is charming but there is no anchorage in the creek as it is full of moorings. Apply to HM at Itchenor or locally on the chance of one being temporarily vacant, but it is possible to dry out alongside the quay by prior permission of the quay master. Otherwise go by dinghy. (7) Anchorage in the Thorney Channel, protected from West winds. At the time of writing there are no facilities as most of the island is RAF property with no public access except by permission, but this may be altered at some future date. (8) Anchorage almost anywhere in the Emsworth Channel on the east side nearly as far as its junction with Sweare Deep, but vessels are not advised to anchor on the west side owing to the mooring area at the southern end and the Fishery Order which covers the remaining area. Pile mooring trots for shoal draught craft beyond the junction light beacon on port side of the Emsworth Channel. At the north end of the channel, which dries out at LW, is the Emsworth Yacht Harbour with pontoon berths. Access over the sill about 1m5 MHWN, 2m7 MHWS.

Port Operation   Port Operation and Information Service VHF (FM) Radio Telephony. Details of these services are available from the HM's Office, Itchenor. Tel: Birdham 512301.

Facilities   At Itchenor there are yacht yards and marine engineers. Landing and water by hose at the floating jetty, where there is a tide-gauge. Diesel oil from the marinas at Birdham but there is a possibility that a fuelling station may be reintroduced at Itchenor. H. C. Darnley & Sons supply chandlery and will fill petrol cans. No shops. The Ship Inn has six bedrooms and a restaurant; some provisions for visitors are available in summer. Occasional buses to Chichester. At Bosham yacht yards and sailmaker, PO and shops. EC Thurs. Buses to Chichester and Portsmouth. In the Emsworth Channel yacht yards at Mengham Rythe and Mill Rythe. Emsworth itself is a small town where there is the yacht harbour and all facilities. EC Wed. Station and buses.

Launching sites: (1) from public hards at end of roads at Itchenor, Bosham and Emsworth, with car parks nearby. (2) Near HW at the north-east side of Hayling Bridge at the slipway administered by the Langstone Sailing Club and also at Dell Quay. (3) at Sandy Point by permission from the Hayling Island S.C. (4) At Emsworth from public hard or Emsworth Yacht Harbour. Yacht clubs: Birdham Y.C., Bosham S.C., Chichester Cruising Club (Itchenor), Chichester Y.C. (Birdham), Dell Quay S.C., Emsworth S.C., Hayling Island S.C., Itchenor S.C., Langstone S.C., Mengham Rythe S.C., West Wittering S.C.

LANGSTONE HARBOUR

Plan Nos. 10a and 10b

High Water +00 h. *14 m. Dover.*
Heights above Datum *at entrance approx. : MHWS 4m9.
MLWS 0m7. MHWN 4m0. MLWN 1m8.*
Depths *Water at entrance varies year by year but there is
1m7 except on east side outside over the hook-shaped bar
extending from the East Winner sand. Within the harbour over
2m in main channels.*

LANGSTONE HARBOUR offers a fine area of water for
dinghies and centreboard boats. There is also plenty of water
for cruising yachts in the main channels, though there are no
deep anchorages immediately off villages with facilities as in
Chichester harbour, nor is it so well buoyed.

Approach and Entrance The entrance to Langstone
Harbour may be located by the high chimney on its west side,
but the channel leading to it lies between the extensive West
Winner and East Winner sands. The R Fairway buoy Gp Fl
(2) W 10 sec. is situated about a mile offshore on Langstone Bar
with a depth of 1m7 on a shoal close north-east of the buoy.
The shoals and sands are liable to alter so that in some years
there may be more water and in other years less. Approach
from the west may be made either from the direction of the
Horse Sand Fort or through the gap in the submerged barrier a
mile north of the fort. If the former, make a position about ½
mile east-north-east of the Horse Sand Fort and bring it into
line with the No Man's Land Fort on a stern transit of 235°
which leads to the buoy. Least water on this course is 1m8, but
a dangerous wreck marked by a green wreck buoy on its south
side must be left to port and there is another wreck (unmarked)
about 3 cables south of the buoy with only 1m2 over it, which

28. *Langstone. The conspicuous chimney and the two dolphins on the west side of the entrance.*

29.   *The northern end of the west side of the entrance channel and ferry pontoon.*

30.   *The northern end of the east side of the entrance channel. White buoys for visitors, HM's office and Ferryboat Inn behind yacht.*

could be a hazard at LW or in rough weather. To avoid it keep close south of the wreck buoy.

If taking the short cut from the Portsmouth direction pass through the gap in the dangerous submerged barrier. The gap lies nearly a mile south of Lumps Fort on the Eastney shore and is marked by a dolphin Qk Fl R on the south side. Keep close to the dolphin in 1m2 as there is an obstruction on the north-north-west side with a buoy on it. Then make good a course of 079° for the Fairway buoy under 2 miles distant, leaving an orange buoy on the north side of the dangerous wreck to starboard.

If approaching from the eastward the danger lies in the East Winner sand, which dries out nearly $\frac{1}{2}$ mile south-east of the Fairway buoy, and has a hook-shaped extension of shoal water with only 0m4 even a mile south-east of the Fairway buoy. The small black conical East Winner buoy is situated about 4 cables south of the shoal. In the absence of local knowledge the buoy should be left to northward and the course should not be altered until the Fairway buoy bears north true which just clears the edge of the East Winner shoal (1m8). Under reasonable conditions Langstone is an easy harbour to enter but the approaches can be dangerous in strong onshore winds, especially near LW on the ebb; it is stated locally that the roughest part of all in southerly winds lies about a cable north-north-east of the Fairway buoy, presumably 2 hours after HW when the ebb is at its maximum rate.

On arrival off the Fairway buoy two dolphins will be seen on the west side of the harbour entrance. The beacons on these dolphins in transit at 344° lead up to the west side of the entrance, but usually a course can be shaped for a position midway between the dolphins and the Hayling Island shore. The edge of the channel to the entrance is steep-to in places on the east side and thus constitutes a danger when the sands are covered at high water. When in the entrance with land on either hand there is plenty of deep water, but the streams run very hard in this bottleneck. Once within the harbour alter course to the desired anchorage. Small craft without masts can pass under Hayling road bridge (2m1 clearance MHWS) to Chichester harbour.

Lights   Fairway buoy Gp Fl (2) W 10 sec. Qk Fl R on outer beacon in entrance and Fl R near Ferry House at north end of the west side of entrance. Three cables within the harbour there are the port hand East Milton buoy Gp Fl (4) R 10 sec. and the starboard hand north-west Sinah buoy Fl W 5 sec.

Anchorage and Facilities   (1) There are four round white visitors' buoys for temporary use on the east side of the entrance near the northern end and just south of the cable beacons. These are adjacent to the HM's office, where enquire about the possibility of a vacant mooring in Sinah Lake or elsewhere. Close by there is a water point for filling cans. There is a boat yard where petrol or diesel fuel can be obtained or direct by dinghy about $1\frac{1}{2}$ hours either side of HW. Other facilities are the Ferry Boat Inn, a café and general store. Launching site at slip. Bus service to Hayling village (EC Wed.) and Havant. Frequent ferries to Eastney in summer, thence bus to Portsmouth. (2) The very active Eastney Cruising Association on east side of entrance (see harbour plan) has two fair-weather visitors' moorings (fierce tide for about an hour about 2 hours after HW); riding light necessary at night. The club is a do-it-yourself concern and hospitable; bar and meals in sailing season. Public launching site at end of road near ferry pontoon. Buses to Portsmouth in summer. (3) Anywhere that can be found on the edges of the main channel out of the fairway (which is used by ballast dredgers) and clear of moorings. (4) Langstone Channel, although far from facilities, provides plenty of room to anchor in depths ranging from 5m0 to 2m0 east of South Binness Island. (5) Eastney Lake dries out and is full of moorings for craft which can take the mud at LW.

31. Eastney Cruising Association club house on west side has two visitors' moorings.

The Locks S.C. has a club house and concrete slip, and there is a general store up the road. Plans have been approved for a marina in Eastney Lake and the development is under consideration.

Launching sites from the foreshore at the end of the roads leading to the ferry on either side of the entrance, preferably at slack water as the tides run very hard. Car parks adjacent. Other yacht club: Tudor S.C. on west of Broom channel.

PORTSMOUTH HARBOUR

Plan No. 11. Admiralty Chart Nos. 2625, 2631

High Water +oo h. 14 m. Dover.
Heights above Datum *MHWS 4m7. MLWS om6. MHWN 3m8. MLWN 1m8. Flood 7 hours. Ebb 5 hours.*
Depths *The entrance and main harbour are a deep ship channel. The Fareham Channel has 7 to 9m at the entrance, gradually shallows, and there is little water off Fareham; Portchester Channel is also deep as far as junction with Tipner Lake but variable in the Portchester reach.*

PRIMARILY a naval port, Portsmouth is not without interest from a yachting point of view. No harbour is better equipped to build or repair yachts, whether large or small, sail or power. It is a safe and convenient port, and the upper reaches and channels provide good small boat sailing and racing. There is a speed limit of 10 knots within 900m of the shore in any part of the dockland port. Water ski-ing is not permitted within the harbour.

Approach and Entrance From the eastward the approach is simple, being buoyed for big ships, and is shown on the chart. From the westward Gilkicker Point should be given a good berth. To keep in deep water, the Spit Sand Fort should be left ¼ mile to port, when course may be altered to the Spit Refuge buoy, whence leaving this to port the deep channel will be followed. A short cut across the Spit Sand, giving 1m8 at low water, can be found ½ mile west of Spit Sand Fort, by keeping the high monument (war memorial) on the Southsea shore in line with St Jude's Church at 048°. Another swashway, available (with sufficient rise of tide above om3 at

32.   Portsmouth. *The leading marks for swashway between Spit and Hamilton Bank are St. Jude's church spire (rear) in line with the war memorial (front). In front of the memorial is the Royal Albert Y.C. signal station.*

33. *The east side of the entrance from the Round Tower to the Ryde ferry terminal and naval dock yard.*

LAT) lies across the Hamilton Bank by keeping the western edge of the Round Tower on east of harbour entrance in line with the western edge of a conspicuous tank at 29½°.

In the entrance itself the tides are very strong, and sailing yachts will find it difficult under contrary conditions. The flood runs easy for 3 hours, strong for 4 hours; the ebb easy 1 hour, strong for from 2 to 3 hours, and then easy.

Vessels approaching inshore from the eastward may pass through the gap in the submerged barrier. The gap is about a mile south of Lumps Fort and is marked by a buoy on the north side and a dolphin (Qk Fl R) on the south. Many of the piles on the barrier have been removed, but the remains and many submerged concrete blocks still constitute a danger.

Fareham Lake About 1½ miles from the entrance, Portsmouth harbour divides into two channels. The westward of the two is Fareham Lake. On the eastern side of the entrance to this creek there are three large stagings known as The Dolphins. A number of mooring buoys are placed on either side in the first reach, and above this the channel is marked by posts on the mud on either bank; red posts to port, black to starboard. Where the Portchester Channel joins the Fareham Channel, do not mistake the first port hand (red) in the Portchester creek for a Fareham mark. At the end of the channel—over 3 miles up—is the town of Fareham, but for a mile below this there is little water at low tide. This part of the channel is not shown on Plan No. 11 beyond the prohibited anchorage, where Heavy Reach turns westward for over ½ mile before turning northward towards Fareham. The channel continues to be marked by piles. Yachts up to 1m8 draught can proceed to Fareham Quay 2 hours either side of HW after passing under power cables with 19m clearance below them.

Portchester Lake This is the eastern arm referred to above. It is a wide channel, running near the entrance in a north-easterly direction, but there are several bends to be negotiated before it leads to the village and the ruins of the castle at Portchester. The navigation marks are the same as in Fareham creek, by posts (red posts port, black starboard) but do not approach these closely. Strangers may find as little as 0m4 LAT in parts of the Portchester reach, particularly west of Nos. 80 & 79 posts. The danger area in Portchester Lake from Tipner Ranges is shown on plan 11. Red flags are flown at the butts when firing is in progress and yachts are requested to pass through the area as quickly as possible.

Lights The approach and entrance to Portsmouth harbour are, of course, clearly marked by lights, which are shown on the chart.

Signals Signals are displayed at Central Signal Station, Fort Blockhouse, or Gilkicker Signal Station or in H.M. ships as appropriate.

1. *Day*. Red flag with white diagonal bar. *Night*. R Lt over two G Lts Vert. No vessel is to leave the harbour or enter the harbour channel from any of the creeks or lakes leading thereto or approach north of Outer Spit buoy.

2. *Day*. Red flag with white diagonal bar over one black ball. No vessel is to enter the harbour channel or approach channel from seaward. Outgoing vessels may proceed.

3. *Day*. One black ball over red flag with white diagonal bar. No vessel shall leave the harbour. Ingoing traffic may use the harbour channel and enter Portsmouth harbour.

4. *Day*. Large black pendant. *Night*. W Lt over two R Lts Vert. No vessel to anchor in the Man-of-War anchorages at Spithead.

5. *Day*. International Code Pendant superior to Pendant zero. Keep clear H.M. ship entering, leaving or shifting berth.

6. *Day*. International Code Pendant superior to Pendant 9. *Night*. Three G Lts Vert. H.M. ship under way. Give wide berth.

7. *Day*. International Code Pendant superior to Flags N E. *Night*. G over R Lt. Proceed with great caution. Ships (other than car ferries) leaving Camber.

8. *Day*. Flag E. *Night*. R over amber Lt. Submarine entering or leaving Haslar lake. Light flashes when submarine under way. Keep clear.

9. *Day*. International Code Pendant superior to Flag A. *Night*. Two R Lts H. Have divers down.

Anchorages, etc. Portsmouth harbour and its approaches are under the jurisdiction of the Queen's Harbour Master, tel. Portsmouth 22351, ext. 2008. Berths from seaward on west side: Haslar lake. No room to anchor, bottom foul. Private moorings mostly for services personnel. Apply to R.N.S.A., or R. Albert Y.C., or Joint Services Sailing Centre adjacent Haslar Bridge, to ask whether a mooring may be temporarily vacant. Small power boats and shoal draught yachts with lowering masts can proceed under the bridge into Alverstoke Lake where there is room to anchor. (2) Camper & Nicholson's Marina. Enquire at fuel barge or visitors' berths at end of No. 3 pontoon. All facilities including building and repairs. Also moorings for very large yachts. (3) Just above C. & N. Marina there are the Gosport Borough yacht moorings in the Cold Harbour with sets of double moorings let annually. Enquire at Gosport boatyard premises on the quay whether a set is temporarily vacant. (4) Gosport Cruising Club, Weevil Lake—apply at Club H.Q. boat for possible temporary mooring. (5) Hardway. All available space occupied by moorings. Hardway Sailing Club is hospitable and welcomes visitors from other clubs; it maintains a trot of five fore and aft visitors' moorings off the pontoon and can advise whether any other moorings are temporarily available. The public hard and pontoon landing stage are the only landing places in the vicinity. Club scrubbing piles and launching site, fuels, chandlery and inn are adjacent with short walk to boatyard, shops, restaurant and buses. (6) On east side of harbour entrance is the Camber. This is a small commercial harbour unsuitable for visiting yachts. Permission to enter and berth must first be obtained from the Dock Master at the entrance. Facilities within include yacht yards, sailmaker and chandlery. (7) Fareham Lake. Anchorage now full of private moorings. Temporary moorings off Wicor marina (and launching site

34. *The entrance to Camper & Nicholson's marina lies between the fuel jetty and the dolphin. The Cold Harbour and Gosport Borough marina lie just beyond Camper & Nicholson's.*

near HW) enquire at yard whether any mooring vacant. Near Fareham Quay, yacht builder, chandler, launching site at public slipway. Shops, banks, hotel, restaurants, etc. at Fareham. EC Wed. Station and buses. (8) With reduction of danger area from Tipner Ranges, Spider Lake and Bomb Ketch Lake are now full of moorings but have no facilities—nearest Hardway or Wicor. (9) Portchester. Anchorage difficult as fairway must be kept clear for hovercraft and all available space near Portchester S.C. is occupied by moorings. Apply to duty officer at club for possibility of temporary use of a mooring. If one is available, the historic castle will be found interesting and facilities are quite good. Club, inn, small shops, club scrubbing and launching site at Portchester hard but often fully booked up and hardly approachable at summer weekends. EC Tues, some Wed. (10) Portsmouth Cruising Club has drying moorings and the usual facilities, but no shops near and ½ mile (0.8 km) walk to buses.

Facilities   At Gosport and Portsmouth there are first-rate facilities and shops of every kind. EC Wed at both towns, Southsea Sat. Express rail service from Portsmouth town or harbour stations. Ferry service to Ryde, I.W., adjacent harbour station, also hovercraft. Car ferries to Wootton, I.W., from Camber. Good bus services. Launching sites: (1) Portsmouth from car ferry slip provided ferries are not obstructed; the position is congested during the summer months. (2) From hard in Gosport Borough marina adjacent to Gosport boatyard office, with very limited public car parking near. (3) At hard of Gosport Cruising Club in Weevil Lake 3 hours either side of HW. Facilities at Hardway, Fareham and Portchester already stated. New public dinghy landing on reclaimed section between C. & N. and Gosport Ferry pontoon. Yacht clubs: R. Albert Y.C. *Ports 25924*, R.N.S.A., *Ports 23524*, Portsmouth S.C., *Ports 20596*, Hardway S.C., *Gosport 81875*, Portsmouth Harbour C.C., *Ports 64337*, Portchester S.C., *Cosham 76375*, Fareham S. & M.B.C., *Fareham 80738*, Gosport C.C.

BEMBRIDGE HARBOUR

Plan No. 12

High Water +*oo h. 14 m. Dover.*
Heights above Datum *in Harbour MHWS 3m1. MHWN
2m3. MLWN 0m4.*

Depths *There are extensive sands which dry at LW but there
is always some water (0m2 to 0m6) left flowing out of the actual
channel. Within the harbour there are depths of 1m3 at the
entrance down to 0m3 in the main channel, but the water is
impounded by the bar from about 1 hour before to 2 hours after low
water springs. Dredged area at St Helen's Marina.*

35. Left *light beacon with tide
gauge at entrance of approach
channel and below St. Helen's
Fort. When coming from seaward
leave the fort about 1½ cables to
port and the beacon about 3 to 3½
metres to starboard.*

BEMBRIDGE is a charming harbour and conveniently situated
for the east end of the island. The marked channel is
approached from the north and lies to the west of St Helen's
Fort. The entrance itself is protected from westerly and
southerly winds. A great handicap is the lack of room for
visiting yachts and the shallowness of the harbour, but there is
a marina at St Helen's.

Approach and Entrance The approach to Bembridge
harbour is made from a north-east direction to a beacon which
is situated 1¾ cables west of St Helen's Fort. The beacon has an
open triangle top and a tide gauge which indicates the least
depth in the channel. It should be left 3 to 4m to starboard as
the channel is only about 9m wide. Then follow the channel
between the buoys, small B Con to starboard and RW Cheq to
port, but do not pass too close to the buoys, especially No. 8.
The channel between this buoy and No. 9 is but narrow,
deeper at No. 11 starboard hand buoy with triangle topmark.
Within the harbour gradually bear to starboard to pass

between No. 13 B buoy and No. 12 RW Cheq buoy and
then follow the shallow buoyed channel to St Helen's.

Lights St Helen's Fort Gp Fl (3) W 10 sec., 16m 8M.
Light beacon west of St Helen's Fort, Qk Fl. Entry at night is
difficult without local knowledge as there are no lights on the
buoys.

Berths, Moorings and Anchorages Anchoring within the harbour is prohibited. Visiting yachts usually proceed up the buoyed fairway which leads to St Helen's quay and the marina, where they lie alongside pontoons dredged for berths giving about 1m2 to 1m8, and considerably more towards Neaps. Large craft can lie alongside St Helen's quay by arrangement and dry out where there is soft mud in parts.

Multi-hull and shoal draught twin-keelers can dry out on the port hand of the entrance, where landings may be made on the beach near the Spithead Hotel, but the area of beach is limited and is soon filled up at weekends during the season.

Moorings for visiting vessels are very limited and are all privately owned. Application should be made to the boatyards before arrival to book one, if they should have any temporarily vacant. Vessels should not pick up vacant moorings without prior arrangement as great confusion is caused if the owners return and there is nowhere for the visitors to move to.

Anchorage outside the harbour is prohibited within 1 cable of St Helen's Fort but can be found to the north of the fort while waiting sufficient rise of tide to enter the channel, or elsewhere according to the vessel's draught and the wind conditions. In offshore winds between west and south there is good anchorage eastward of Bembridge off Under Tyne outside local moorings, but the landing is rough and it is ½ mile (0.8 km) walk to the harbour.

Facilities There are several good yacht yards within the harbour and marine engineers. Water by hose and diesel oil, etc. at marina, with Brading Harbour Y.C. adjacent (which welcomes temporary members); shops and PO ¼ mile (0.4 km) distant at St Helen's. Diesel oil is also supplied by Harbour Engineering at the sheds ¼ mile east of the B.H.Y.C. and both diesel and petrol at their embankment premises next to Coombes yard.

At Bembridge itself there are the Spithead Hotel and other hotels and restaurants, small shops, EC Thurs. Buses to all parts of the Island. Launching sites at concrete ramp near St Helen's seamark, or by arrangement with yacht yards or clubs. Yacht clubs: Bembridge S.C., Brading Harbour Y.C.

WOOTTON CREEK

Plan No. 13

High Water *+ oo h. 14 m. Dover.*
Heights above Datum *MHWS 4m5. MLWS om7.*
MHWN 3m6. MLWN 1m7.
Depths *The channel is dredged to 2m4 up to the ferry slipway. Basin dries LAT on soft mud. In the river there is only om6 to om3.*

WOOTTON CREEK is pretty and for small craft the entrance is normally easy to identify and navigate. Like other sailing ports it suffers from over-popularity, resulting in difficulty in finding room to bring up during summer weekends.

Approach and Entrance The entrance to the Creek is clearly marked by an outer pile and three dolphins. Strangers should steer for the outer pile, leaving this and the other three dolphins to starboard. The dredged channel is very narrow and very busy in summer months; yachts should not impede the entering or leaving ferries as they cannot alter course out of the dredged channel. When the yacht comes to the third dolphin she may stand on for the end of the ferry pier, leaving this very close to port and with sufficient rise of tide enter the bight situated north-west of the ferry pier. Here she will find anchorage and moorings belonging to the Royal Victoria Yacht Club with Berthing Master in attendance. Visiting yachtsmen are welcome.

If (again with sufficient rise of tide) it is desired to sail up the river, proceed from No. 3 dolphin steering for the ferry pier until the small BW starboard hand buoy is abeam, then turn on transit of leading marks, which consist of two white triangles on the west foreshore near a boathouse. The channel is marked by BW buoys to starboard and RW buoys to port until the first bend. The channel is narrow and strangers should be careful not to run on to or cross the finger of mud shown on the harbour plan on the port side of the channel between the Creek channel and the Bight moorings. A RW buoy sits on this spit. Vessels proceeding past the first bend in the river near the leading marks should follow the moored craft, leaving them close to starboard. There are a slip and dinghy park on the starboard side of the Creek just south of the boat yards.

Lights The outer pile beacon and second dolphin Fl W 6 sec. First and third dolphins Fl G 6 sec.

Anchorage There is reasonable anchorage in settled weather and offshore winds outside the Creek to north-west of the pile beacon at the entrance. Within the Creek the only anchorage for boats up to say 1m5 lies in the bight beyond the ferry pier. Here it dries out at LAT, but yachts sit upright in very soft mud. Anchors should be buoyed and it is essential to anchor clear of the car ferry fairway and where the ferries turn to their hard. There are also many moorings but it is best to obtain advice from the Berthing Master, who usually meets incoming yachts and directs them to a berth.

Shallow draught vessels, which can take the mud, will find room to anchor up river, but there are many moorings in the best parts. Advice can be obtained from the Berthing Master.

Facilities At Fishbourne there are an inn and garage, and the R. Victoria Y.C. club house. This club has good facilities with hard, car park, changing rooms, bar and club boatman. Visiting yachts are welcome and temporary membership is available to members of recognized yacht clubs. At Wootton, $\frac{3}{4}$ mile up the river or a mile's (1.6 km) walk from Fishbourne, there are three boatyards, garage (water and petrol), PO, shops, inn. EC Thurs. Launching sites: from ferry hard or yacht club by arrangement. Frequent buses from Wootton Bridge to Ryde and Newport.

COWES

Plan No. 14

High Water +*oo h. 14 m. Dover.*
Heights above Datum *MHWS 4m2. MLWS om6. MHWN 3m5. MLWN 1m7.*
Depths *The bed of the River Medina is uneven but there is upwards of 1m8 in the fairway from the entrance as far up as Medham beacon, situated 4 cables beyond Kingston Quay.*

COWES remains the principal yachting racing centre of the British Isles, and is the headquarters of the Royal Yacht Squadron. It is a town of tradition and character that time has little changed. Situated in the centre of the Island coast opposite the entrance of Southampton Water, it is the most conveniently placed harbour in the Solent. There is always room to bring up, and the harbour is well protected except from the northward.

Approach and Entrance The entrance is a particularly simple one and well marked. The fairway lies on the west side of the entrance, and is marked by the port hand RW (No. 4) light buoy (Fl R 5 sec.) and the starboard hand B Con (No. 3)

36. The Royal Yacht Squadron castle is conspicuous on the west side of the entrance to Cowes.

37. The Island Sailing Club and pontoon on left with the Customs Office just to the right.

buoy; in the harbour there are two R port hand buoys of which no. 8 is Qk Fl R.

Approaching from the east, to clear the Shrape Mud near LW steer to the Trinity House buoy, B W H S (Fl Or 2 sec.) and then keep on the line from the buoy to the north side of the Royal Yacht Squadron castle until the fairway is entered. The R.Y.S. castle stands out conspicuously on the north-west corner of the entrance. A long breakwater extends across the Shrape bank, with the object of forcing the tide to scour the channel, thus preventing silting. There is little water to the north of this breakwater, but liberties can be taken (and almost always are when racing) when there is sufficient rise of tide. A

special hovercraft fairway on the east side of the harbour and close round the end of the breakwater is marked by red buoys. Yachts crossing this hovercraft channel and its approach should exercise caution.

Coming from the west, there is deep water a cable offshore but there are ledges of rock east of Egypt Point and off the shore along Cowes Green to the Royal Yacht Squadron. Leave No. 3 outer B buoy to starboard. Note that an early flood or ebb which runs contrary to the main tide will be found between Egypt Point and the Royal Yacht Squadron.

There is a speed limit of 6 knots, but yachts must slow down below this in vicinity of other yachts on moorings or as

38. Cowes Yacht Haven Marina is close south of the Fountain Pier. Enter at south end near the buoy.

seamanship requires.

Lights The Prince Consort buoy, north-east of the entrance, exhibits a Qk Fl W Lt, and there is a Lt (Fl R ev 5 sec.) on the outer (No. 4) port hand buoy. A R Qk Fl Lt is placed on the end of the eastern breakwater. Leading lights at 164° are: Front Iso 2 sec., Rear Iso R 2 sec. The rear R Lt is visible 120° to 240°. The principal lights in the River Medina are shown on the harbour plan.

Anchorage, Moorings and Marinas Large yachts anchor or moor on buoys provided in the roads north of the Shrape bank, or on moorings off Cowes esplanade. Smaller yachts anchor on the Shrape well to the north-west of the breakwater and local moorings in positions depending upon their draught, remembering that at MLWS there is 0m6 and at MLWN 1m7 more water than shown at chart datum. Anchor should be buoyed to avoid fouling mooring chains.

Four large visitors' moorings are laid off Cowes esplanade for temporary use. There are many private moorings in The Hole on the east side of the harbour and north-west of it. Additional moorings are laid for the various classes of competitors in Cowes Week and other regattas. None should be picked up without permission of the HM, who should always be consulted.

Anchorages are rough in strong northerly winds, as also berths on moorings in the main harbour. In northerly gales it is better to enter one of the marinas or proceed up the river beyond the floating bridge where there are visitors' pile moorings for any size of yacht.

The Cowes Yacht Haven Marina (depths 0m9 to 2m3) is situated on the starboard hand just beyond the Fountain pier and the Red Funnel pontoon in the main channel. Outside this there are mooring buoys and two trots of pile moorings where yachts lie abreast in over 2m. The Willment Marina is situated about 3 cables above the floating bridge on the port hand. It is

39. The Folly Inn on the east bank of the River Medina. There are pile moorings opposite it.

dredged to provide berths from 2m0 to 3m0.

The depths in the river above the floating bridge vary as shown on the harbour plan and in greater detail on Admiralty Chart 2793, but there is 1m8 as far as Medham beacon situated some 4 cables beyond Kingston Quay. There are many pile moorings on either side of the river; all, including those for visitors, are suitably labelled.

A pleasant part in which to bring up is on pile moorings off the Folly Inn in 0m6, which gives 1m4 at MLWS or 2m3 at MLWN. There are a landing pontoon and a restaurant and small shop at the inn. Half a mile to the south on the east side is the Wight Marina in which there are berths for yachts up to about 2m0 maximum draught. The river dries out but with sufficient rise of tide the lock can be reached. At HW the river

is navigable to Newport with the aid of the Admiralty chart.

Facilities Every kind of yachting requirement is catered for. There are yacht yards, sailmakers, brokers, yacht chandlers, hotels and restaurants, Customs, bonded stores and many shops of all kinds including yachting outfitters. EC Wed. Bus connections to all parts. Ferry steamer, hydrofoil and hovercraft to Southampton. Yacht clubs: Royal Yacht Squadron, R. London Y.C., R. Corinthian Y.C., Island S.C., East Cowes S.C., Cowes Corinthian Y.C. Launching sites: (1) From the slipway off the esplanade near Island Sailing Club, with car park adjacent. (2) From the slipway on town quay adjacent to the ferry pontoon, but car parking restricted. (3) Heavy boats can be craned into the water from British Road Services jetty by arrangement.

HAMBLE RIVER

Plan No. 15

Double High Water *First HW Springs approx. – 00 h. 20 m. Dover.*

Heights above Datum *at Calshot Castle MHWS 4m4. MLWS 0m6. MHWN 3m6. MLWN 1m8.*

Depths *3m6 in entrance, and upwards of 2m1 in the channel as far as Mercury Yacht Harbour. Above this 1m5 will be found to Bursledon bridge, and in parts this depth is exceeded.*

THE HAMBLE RIVER owes its popularity as a yachting centre to its convenience and facilities. Situated at the entrance of Southampton Water, it is a good harbour from which cruises may be made to the various Solent and cross-channel ports, and it is a base for many offshore and racing yachts. The channel is available at all states of the tide, but outside the fairway it is packed solid with moorings as far as Bursledon bridge and even beyond it.

Approach and Entrance On coming abreast of Calshot Castle alter course to 350°. The vessel will leave to starboard the Hook pillar bell buoy (Qk Fl W) (which is situated in the centre of Southampton Water) and the course leads to Hamble Point buoy, Sph BW H S (Fl W 7 sec.).

When approaching from the eastward keep well offshore, leaving the Coronation buoy a cable to starboard and steering nothing east of Hamble Point buoy until this is close at hand.

Hamble Point buoy marks the southern extremity of a sand and mud spit on the west side of the Hamble River. The spit dries out for a considerable distance at LW and on the east side of the river there is an almost equally large expanse of mud.

Leaving Hamble Point buoy close to port bring the port hand No. 6 beacon in transit with a conspicuous red roof at 344½°. Then a cable below the beacon alter course to the next transit which is Warsash Shore beacon (on the starboard hand beyond Warsash jetty) in line with a beacon on the Rising Sun on the same side as the beacon at 024½°. However, none but large yachts need use these transits by day as the channel is well marked by four red piles with can topmarks on the port hand and to starboard by five black piles with triangle topmarks. Keep on the starboard hand under power or with a free wind and do not pass too close to the piles, some of which dry out.

In the river above Warsash the fairway is obvious by reference to the harbour plan and the lines of yachts on moorings and piles.

Lights Hamble Point Fl W 7 sec. First transit; front, No. 6 Pile beacon Gp Occ (2) W 12 sec. in line with rear, Hamble beacon Qk Fl R. A cable before reaching No. 6 Pile beacon come on to next transit: front, Warsash Shore beacon Qk Fl W and rear, Rising Sun beacon Iso, R 6 sec. at 024½°. Above Warsash the river is marked by lights on piles as shown on the harbour plan: Qk Fl R to port and Qk Fl W to starboard.

Anchorage, Moorings, Marinas There is no room left for anchoring except temporarily below No. 9 starboard hand pile near the edges of the channel clear of the transit line. Rough in strong south-west wind against a spring ebb.

Application should be made to the HM at Hamble for berthing, which is available for visiting yachts in the following positions marked by notices. (1) Warsash: Piles on port hand opposite Morgan Giles yard. (2) Hamble: Pile moorings for large and small yachts on the starboard side opposite Port Hamble Marina. Berths temporarily vacant can sometimes be found on application to yacht clubs by members of affiliated clubs or to yacht yards.

Application can be made for a vacant berth to the marina HM at any of the marinas—see harbour plan: Fairey's Yacht

40.   The Hamble River is the most concentrated yacht centre in the British Isles, with marinas and facilities of every kind. (Photo : Aerofilms Ltd.)

Harbour pontoon on west side of entrance. Pontoons also at Port Hamble Marina, Mercury Yacht Harbour about half way up the river on port side and Swanwick Marina on the starboard hand.

Facilities   Customs Office at Hamble, bonded stores can be arranged. Water and fuel at marinas or yacht yards and supply boat in river. Yacht builders and repair yards, marine engineers and chandlers at Warsash, Hamble, Swanwick and Bursledon and at marinas. Three hards available for scrubbing against piles: Warsash, Mercury and Land's End hards. Sailmakers at Sarisbury (Bruce Banks Ltd) and J. R. Williams at Hamble. Proctors Metal Masts at Swanwick. Banks at Hamble and one at Warsash. Restaurants, shops and PO's at Hamble, Warsash, Bursledon and Swanwick. EC Wed. except Warsash Thurs. Hotel and restaurant Hamble, Warsash and Bursledon. Launching sites: (1) Warsash public hard, car park adjacent. (2) Hamble public hard, car park adjacent. (3) Swanwick Shore public hard (next to Moody's yacht yard) with car park adjacent. (4) At Bursledon on south-west side of bridge and at Land's End public hard with car park at station ¼ mile (0.4 km) distant. Buses from Warsash, Hamble, Swanwick and Bursledon. Station at Bursledon. Yacht clubs: R. Southern Y.C., R. Thames Y.C., Household Division Y.C. Hamble River S.C., Warsash S.C.

Plan Nos. 16 and 17. Admiralty Chart Nos. 1905 and 2041

Double High Water *First HW Springs* −00 h. *13 m. Dover. 'Young Flood' stand lasts from 1½ to 3 hours after local LW.*
Heights above Datum *MHWS 4m5. MLWS 0m5. MHWN 3m7. MLWN 1m8.*
Depths *Deep harbour for ships with draughts up to 50m2.*

SOUTHAMPTON WATER is a natural harbour which has been used by ships of all kinds from time immemorial. It is an almost straight stretch of water, measuring some 6 miles from Calshot Castle to the Royal pier. Navigation is straightforward by day or night in well buoyed channels and, notwithstanding that Southampton is primarily a commercial port, there are also anchorages available for yachts, although they are generally remote from facilities. The city is an administrative centre and provides almost everything required by yachtsmen.

Approach and Entrance When entering Southampton Water strangers will, of course, be nagivating from a chart of the Solent. It will be seen that the main channel lies between Calshot Spit buoy and Calshot pillar buoy, and runs northwest close to Calshot Castle.

Approaching from the eastward keep well offshore between Hill Head and Hamble, as the shoal water extends a surprisingly long way from the shore. Whether coming from east or west remember the Bramble Bank, situated in mid-Solent. In spite of being such a well-known danger, yachts still occasionally go ashore on this shingle shoal which may vary year to year in depth and position.

41. Approaching Southampton Water. Calshot Castle to right, Fawley Power Station chimney to left.

Once within Southampton Water navigation is easy. Mud flats run off a long way on the western side, and on the eastern side at the southern end (Hamble Spit and Bald Head) and the Weston Shelf at the north-east end. The deep ship channel is marked by red buoys on the west side, and by black conical buoys on the east side.

The docks will be seen from a considerable distance. Here there is the Port Signal and Radar Station at the junction of two channels, the Test river leading approximately north-west, and the Itchen River joining from north-north-east. The Test is the main clearly marked channel leading past the Ocean Dock, the Royal pier and the long line of the Western Docks leading to the Container berths.

Alternatively, if proceeding to moorings or farther up the River Test, the Marchwood Channel may be taken. The entrance lies just north of the Middle Swinging Ground No. 2 R can buoy about 3 cables west-north-west of the Royal pier.

The leading beacons will then be brought into transit at 298°. The front one is a white triangle on a dolphin and the rear a white diamond on a dolphin. The depth on the transit is 2m4 to within ½ cable of the front beacon. Close to starboard lies a long shoal marked on its far north-east side by a beacon and a pile. On the port hand from No. 2 buoy to Marchwood buoy there is shoal water almost as far as Husband's jetty, where it deepens to 2m and more for 3 cables. There are a great many moorings in this area. The shoal area in the Marchwood Channel lies from about ½ cable south-east of the first beacon nearly as far as the rear beacon and both beacons should be left close to port. There are many small craft moorings in the area in depths of 0m5 to 0m9. Immediately after passing the rear beacon a vessel is in deep water of the main channel dredged to 10m2, leading past the Container berths and Swinging Ground.

The Eling Channel, which is very narrow and dries out, is entered close south to the North-west Swinging Ground

42.   Dock head and Port Signal and Radar Station at the junction of Test River to left and Itchen River to right.

(Eling) buoy. It is marked by beacons with triangle topmarks on the starboard hand except at the junction with the Redbridge Channel, which is marked by a junction beacon BRW. Near the entrance of Eling Channel there are two port hand beacons, south of which there are small craft moorings in 0m3. Power cables cross the channel, height 36m.

The River Itchen is commercialized in its lower reaches up to and beyond the Northam bridge, and is used by yachts when proceeding to yacht yards and terminal situated in the river. At the entrance the wide drying flats of Weston Shelf are left to starboard and the dredged area for the docks and basins is on the port side. Beyond the dredged area the channel carries 2m6 past the new Itchen bridge at Woolston as far as the end of the line of big moorings buoys ½ mile beyond the bridge. In this reach there is the port hand Crosshouse beacon (Occ R) and to starboard the Chapel beacon (Fl W). Beyond these the channel runs between wide mud flats on either hand and the depths are

variable up to Camper & Nicholsons, so that in the absence of local knowledge the depth is 1m1 which gives 1m6 at MLWS.

Lights   Calshot Spit buoy exhibits a Lt Gp Fl (2) W5 sec. Electric fog signal 2 ev 60 sec., and the Calshot pillar buoy, Fl W 3 sec., bell 30 sec. The entrance between the two is thus as easy by night as by day. Southampton Water is marked by buoys with R Occ or R Fl Lts on the port side and W Fl or Occ Lts on the starboard. The lights are so numerous that reference to the plan or to chart should be made.

Port Signal and Radar Station   Call sign SPR (Southampton Port Radio) is available for communication on VHF R/T Channel Nos. 16, 14 & 12.

Anchorages   Where available these are generally remote from facilities, but it is possible in suitable weather conditions to anchor anywhere that can be found in Southampton Water clear of (a) prohibited areas, (b) shipping fairways and docks and their approaches and (c) moorings. If near the last the

43. The rear beacon in the end of the Marchwood channel. In background are the container berths to be left to starboard if proceeding up the Eling channel. The picture was taken against the light.

anchor should be buoyed. A riding light is necessary at night. Some of the positions for anchorage or moorings are: (1) Between Calshot Castle and Fawley RW buoy temporary anchorage off the mud flats in moderate west to south-west winds. Far from facilities. (2) Hythe. Large yachts lie north and south of Hythe pier. For smaller craft enquire at yacht yard or club for moorings, or anchor south of the pier. Yacht yard, hotel, shops, petrol, etc. EC Wed. (3) Southampton. There are Harbour Board moorings for large yachts off the Royal pier. (4) Marchwood. Many moorings south of the Marchwood Channel. Enquire at Husband's shipyard or

Marchwood Y.C., failing which find anchorage. Fuel and water at shipyard jetty and frequent launches to Southampton Town Quay. (5) Container Swinging Ground. Anchorage prohibited but at Neaps there is just room to anchor close beyond No. 14 and the Eling buoys. Far from facilities. (6) River Itchen. There are Harbour Board moorings for large yachts and on the east side of the river almost opposite Camper & Nicholsons there is Kemp's Shipyard who own the yacht terminal with alongside berths (2m0 at MLWS and soft bottom) with fuelling, water and chandlery. Anchorage is possible in the Itchen River on the starboard hand out of the main fairway but serves little useful purpose. (7) Netley. Off the hard ½ mile north-west of Netley dome and to north-west between small craft moorings and hovercraft testing area marked by BlW buoys. Yacht yard at hard. Lee shore in prevailing winds.

Other Facilities Southampton, like Portsmouth, provides facilities of almost every kind for yachts, large or small. Ministry of Transport office. Customs and bonded stores. Weather Centre. Camper & Nicholsons large yacht builders and shipyard (also marine engineers yacht agents, chart agency, compass adjusting, instruments and chandlery) and smaller yards and boat-builders. Shops of all kinds, EC Mon. some Wed. Hotels, restaurants, car ferry service, hydrofoil and hovercraft to Cowes. Good train services including express 70 minutes to London. Buses to all parts.

Launching sites (1) From foreshore north of Hythe pier, (2) from ramp at head of Ashlett Creek, south of oil refineries, (3) from hard on north shore of Eling Creek, (4) Itchen River at Woolston hard on east side or up river at Kemp's Shipyard, (5) at public hard, Netley. Yacht clubs: R. Southampton Y.C., Southampton S.C., Eling S.C., Weston S.C., Hythe S.C., Marchwood Y.C., Esso S.C., Netley Cliff S.C.

BEAULIEU RIVER

Plan No. 18

Double High Water *at entrance. First HW Springs* −*oo h.*
30 m. Dover.

Heights above Datum *at entrance approx. MHWS 3m7.*
MLWS om6. MHWN 3m1. MLWN 1m6.

Depths   *About om6 LAT on the bar; within the river the*
depths are variable as shown on the plan and, except near LW
springs, there is 1m8 up to the yacht harbour at Buckler's Hard
and considerably more water in parts of the river.

BEAULIEU RIVER provides one of the most beautiful
anchorages within the Solent. A long, straight channel leads
between the mud flats to the river proper, most of which lies
between deep woods on either hand. The entrance is well
marked, and is available to most vessels except at exceptionally
low spring tides.

Approach and Entrance   From the west follow the line
of the Hampshire coast, keeping well away from the mud flats,
until the tripod beacon, Qk Fl R, at the eastern end of Beaulieu
Spit, the Lepe Coastguard cottages and a conspicuous white
boathouse have been identified. Continue until the leading
marks come into line at 339°. The front is a white board with a
triangular top at the summit of the first port hand pile, and the
rear, which is situated among dark green trees, has a similar
white board with a triangular top but with the addition of a
vertical black stripe in the centre. Follow their transit which
leaves the dolphin a few metres to port across a bar with om6.

44.   *Entrance of Beaulieu River. Tripod beacon on left, white leading marks centre and former coastguard cottages to right.*

45. *Yacht Harbour and Bucklers Hard. (Photo: Aerofilms Ltd.)*

Within the entrance the river soon deepens and it is marked by red piles with can tops and red reflectors (even numbers) on the port hand and black piles (odd numbers) with conical tops and white reflectors to starboard. About a cable off the inner beacon there is a sharp bend in the river to the west-south-west; the turn is well marked by piles.

From the eastward leave three Qk Fl R beacons to starboard. After passing the third do not steer direct to Beaulieu Spit dolphin near LW springs, but steer to come on the leading transit at over 2 cables south of the beacon.

Once beyond the first bend the channel continues to be marked by pile beacons and it is fairly wide to the next bend at

Need's Oar Point. Above this point the river is marked by perches. There are a few shoal patches as shown on the plan which require attention at LW springs but at most states of the tide vessels of, say, 1m8 draft have no difficulty in sailing up to the Yacht Harbour and ¼ mile beyond it.

Swashway Bull Lake, as it is known, provides a short cut off Need's Oar Point when coming from the westward. It dries out at LW but carries about 2m4 at MHWS, and is usually marked by two small round red buoys to port and three black to starboard. Approach the outer buoys from about south-west—not across the flats east or west.

Light Beaulieu Spit beacon Qk Fl R. Vis 277°–037°.

Anchorage Owing to the large numbers of moorings, yachts may anchor only in the long reach between the prohibited anchorage west of the entrance and Need's Oar Point.

There are pile moorings near Buckler's Hard to accommodate about 100 visiting yachts, and other moorings temporarily vacant can sometimes be had on application to the HM, whose office is at the Yacht Harbour Marina. Here there are berths for seventy-six yachts and a yacht yard.

Facilities Water and fuel at the pier at Buckler's Yard or at the Yacht Harbour. At Buckler's Hard there are the Master Builder's Hotel, the Maritime Museum and a good village stores, with deep freeze, which opens every day. There is also a taxi service. Launching site at Buckler's Hard or from beach at Lepe opposite the entrance to the river; both with convenient car parks. Yacht clubs: Beaulieu River S.C. and R. Southampton Y.C. at Ginn's Farm. Nearest stations Beaulieu Road, or Brockenhurst 6 miles (9.6 km).

NEWTOWN RIVER

Plan No. 19

Double High Water *First HW Springs approx. —00 h. 30 m. Dover.*

Heights above Datum *MHWS 3m4. MLWS 0m5. MHWN 2m8. MLWN 1m5.*

Depths *About 0m9 on the bar, then 3m3 to Fishhouse Point. Within the harbour from 1m2 to 0m9 as far as Causeway Lake.*

THE VILLAGE of Newtown is one of the smallest in the Isle of Wight. Once it was the capital, and vessels of all sizes used the river as a harbour. Romans sacked the town, and then in 1377 it was burnt to the ground by the French. Today there is little except the old town hall (now National Trust property) and cuttings through the trees, where once ran roads, to hint of its former importance. But the river still remains, and where once lay fourteenth-century sailing ships one now sees yachts and boats. Although the anchorage is crowded in weekends during the season, the river, the marshlands and woods retain much of their original character. The National Trust owns the Estuary and much of the adjoining land and marshes which are the nesting places of countless sea birds. Landing at Fishhouse Point is not allowed during the nesting season, April to June.

Approach and Entrance The entrance to Newtown River is 3½ miles east of Yarmouth and lies eastward of Hamstead Point, which is the most pronounced headland between Yarmouth and Gurnard. It will be identified with certainty when the Hamstead Ledge black conical buoy is sighted. The bar lies ¾ mile east-south-east of this buoy.

As the entrance is approached the leading marks will be

46.   *Newtown River. Within the entrance leave well to starboard the shingle bank marked by green perches and temporarily by a visitor. Then gradually bear to starboard in the channel marked by perches and by the line of yachts at anchor or moorings in the centre of it.*

seen, although they are not very conspicuous. They stand on the shore east of the entrance and consist of two posts, the outer one RW with a white 'Y' topmark and the inner one a white disc within a black ring. Alter course to stand in on these marks, and allow for strong athwart ship tide. Leave the bar buoy (R Sph) to port and the second (B Sph) marking a gravel spit projecting towards the channel, to starboard. When the 'Y' post is close ahead (do not approach it closely at LW), alter course for the entrance between the shingle points. There are a few perches on each side of the channel with red can topmarks to port and green painted ones to starboard. Here the tide conforms to the direction of the channel, running either in or out.

Soon the entrance will be at hand. To starboard there is a shingle spit which is fairly steep-to, but beyond it is mud, whilst on the port hand a little farther in is another fairly steep shingle point, known as Fishhouse Point. Beyond this the channel divides; the port hand one is Clamerkin Lake, but the main channel is straight ahead and runs in a southerly direction.

There is a nasty reef of gravel to starboard opposite the junction of Clamerkin Lake and the main river, marked by three B booms, so keep to port after entering, before sweeping round into the centre of the river. In this reach there are usually yachts on moorings or at anchor which show the lay of the channel, and a few perches. Here the channel is very narrow at LW.

Anchorage The principal anchorage is between the junction of the main channel with Clamerkin Lake (where there is 2m7) and the junction with Causeway Lake ¼ mile farther south, where there is about 1m0 at LW. Several moorings occupy the best positions in about 1m8, so that the visitor will have to anchor where best he can, nearer the entrance according to what space is available. The anchorage is rather exposed to north-east winds. Alternatively, there is anchorage at the lower end of Clamerkin Lake in 1m2 and rather more water farther up the lake where there are moorings, two of which are for visitors. There is danger from rifle practice near the head of the lake. Moorings can often be hired on application to the HM. Dues are charged to help with cost of upkeep of river and moorings; if not collected put a suitable coin in the box beside the boathouse. Smaller craft that can take the mud at LW will find room farther up the main channel. There are no lights on the river at night.

Facilities Water at tap at south end of footbridge and Lower Hamstead farm. Farm produce from farms at Shalfleet or Newtown, but there are no shops at Newtown and facilities are limited, so it is best to stock provisions beforehand.

There are a small slip and boatyard at Lower Hamstead (K. W. Marshall) and another small yard (R. Woodford) at Shalfleet Quay. There is no station but a weekday post bus from Newtown to Newport 0930 returning 1230. Shalfleet is 2 miles from the anchorage. Go by dinghy to Shalfleet village, where there is a bus service to Newport and Yarmouth. There are a small shop and inn. Petrol, diesel and paraffin at Shalfleet Service Station on main road. If possible go up on the flood and return on the ebb.

YARMOUTH HARBOUR

Plan No. 20

Double High Water *First HW Springs —00 h. 51 m. Dover.*
Heights above Datum *MHWS 3m1. MLWS 0m6. MHWN 2m5. MLWN 1m4.*
Depths *Tide gauges are placed on the pier facing north for incoming vessels and on the dolphin facing south for vessels leaving the harbour. There is 1m3 in the entrance and from 2m3 to 1m3 within the harbour itself.*

YARMOUTH provides a good protected harbour available to yachts at all states of the tide. The town itself is a beautiful one, especially viewed from seaward. It provides what in some respects is the most popular port in the Solent; so much so that yachts have sometimes to be refused entry in summer weekends.

Approach and Entrance   Yarmouth can be located from a considerable distance by its conspicuous pier. There is plenty of water in the approaches from east or west off the pierhead, but there is a local tide rip situated near the Black Rock (marked by black conical buoy) about 4 cables to the westward of Yarmouth pier. With sufficient rise of tide small craft can pass inside the Black Rock (dries 0m8) by keeping the end of the Victoria pier (a cable east of Sconce Point) in line with the south side of Hurst Castle. This passage carries 0m4 but do not go north of the line until Black Rock has been passed.

The harbour entrance lies just to the west of the pier, and there are leading marks, consisting of two posts surmounted by white diamonds with two horizontal black lines, which indicate the best water in the approach channel. At the entrance there are a large dolphin (used for warping the ferry under bad conditions) close to the end of the breakwater on the starboard hand and the ferry jetty on the port hand. Best water will be found by keeping on the port side off the jetty but stand out to avoid the slipway at its inner end and bear to starboard

47.   *The entrance with Yarmouth Castle to port and a dolphin and the breakwater to starboard.*

48. *After passing the dolphin bear to starboard to the lettered line and numbered pile moorings as directed by the Harbour Master.*

towards the rows of piles. The HM usually gives berthing instructions from the quay, but yachts should have warps and fenders ready for mooring temporarily. The harbour is dredged to allow for rows of pile moorings, between which are narrow fairways and depths range from 2m2 to 1m3. There is little room for a yacht to tack, and most use auxiliary power, or warp into position. Motor yachts should reduce speed. When the harbour is full a red flag is hoisted at a flagpole at the seaward end of the ferry jetty at the harbour entrance, or at night two R Lts Vert are exhibited from the same point. Yachts may then enter only with permission of the HM.

Lights There are fixed lights at the end of the long outer pier. F G Lts are placed on the two leading marks. There is a F R Lt (and two W when a ferry is expected) at the end of the ferry jetty which is left to port when entering, after which course is gradually altered to starboard into the harbour.

Moorings and Anchorage Yachts berth alongside each other, moored stem and stern to the mooring piles provided for the purpose. The HM will indicate which berth to take. Each line of piles has a letter and each pile a number. There is no anchorage in the harbour, but above the swing bridge (arrange time to open with HM) there is some room left clear of moorings in which to anchor in the river. Outside there is anchorage to west or east of the end of the pier, although the swell from passing ships causes temporary discomfort, and the anchorage is exposed to northerly winds. Bring up a little inside the line of the pier end if draught permits.

Facilities There are three yacht yards, marine engineer and scrubbing berths. Good yacht chandler and ironmongery. Water and fuel at New Quay, petrol also at chandlers. Customs Office next to HM. Yarmouth is a compact little town with hotels and restaurants. Quay St shops include chandler, PO and bookseller. EC Thurs. Dinghy compound. Launching sites from dinghy slips at the Quay or from the ferry slip by arrangement with the HM; car park adjacent. Frequent car ferries to Lymington. Buses to Newport and connections with all parts. Yacht club: R. Solent Y.C.

LYMINGTON

Plan No. 21

Double High Water *First HW Springs −00 h. 41 m. Dover.*

Heights above Datum *MHWS 3m0. MLWS 0m5. MHWN 2m6. MLWN 1m3.*

Depths *1m4 outside the entrance, then 2m4 in mid-channel to the Ferry Terminal. Depths then decrease to 0m9 off the Town Quay with a 0m3 shoal a cable short of it.*

LYMINGTON RIVER provides a good harbour available to most yachts at all states of the tide. It is a pleasant place in which to bring up. Lymington itself is a small and charming Hampshire town, which provides yachtsmen with excellent facilities of every kind. As a yachting centre it has developed greatly with big marinas and two very active yacht clubs which have made it one of the most important racing centres in the Solent.

Approach and Entrance The entrance lies about 2½ miles north-east of Hurst Castle. Whether approaching from west or east keep well away from the extensive mud flats and shoal water. The first mark which will probably be identified is the starting platform for races on the east side of the entrance. Incoming or outgoing car ferries assist in pilotage and on nearer approach the historic outer Jack-in-the Basket beacon at the mouth of the river on its port side will be seen. The R. Lymington club house 1¼ miles up the river is also conspicuous. Once the entrance has been identified the rest is easy, as the winding channel is clearly marked by red piles on the port hand and black piles with white triangles or barrels on the starboard. There are two pairs of leading beacons on the mud in the Short Reach for the ferries. The only hazards are these big car ferries which have very little room to manœuvre in the channel at LW and have right of way. They are very well handled and surprisingly few accidents occur.

Lights Two red leading lights on pylons lead to the entrance at 318°, but it is better for yachts to follow the lights on the beacons: five Fl R or Qk Fl R to port and seven Fl W to starboard. Qk Fl amber at ferry terminal.

Anchorage Anchorage is prohibited in the river, which is

49.   *The Royal Lymington Y.C. starting platform is conspicuous on the starboard side of the river entrance.*

50. *Entrance to Lymington Yacht Haven Marina in Harper's Lake.*

fully occupied by Lymington Harbour Commissioners' moorings. These should not be picked up without permission. Arrangements for berthing, particularly for large yachts, should be made with the HM. There are berths for upwards of 100 visiting yachts apart from marinas, and the following are the principal positions: (1) On mooring buoys below the

51. Royal Lymington Yacht Club. The main channel to the Berthon shipyard and marina is on extreme right.

bridge, where there is about 0m9, but a soft bottom so that the keel sinks into the mud and yachts remain upright at low water. (2) Alongside Custom House quay, 50m long, up to about six abreast. About 0m9 alongside to 1m3 some 6m from the quay, i.e., third berth out. (3) Berths are sometimes temporarily vacant at the marinas, the Berthon Boat Co., Ltd or Lymington Yacht Haven in Harper's Lake. (4) Anchorage outside river is possible in offshore winds and settled weather.

Facilities   These are outstandingly good. First-class yacht builders and repairers for all sizes of yachts. Leading international sailmakers for ocean racing and other classes and two smaller sailmakers. Customs. Brooks & Gatehouse electronics. Water at Bath Road pontoon and Town Quay and at marina pontoons where fuel is also available. Hotels, restaurants, inns, banks and shops of all kinds. EC Wed. Stations at Ferry Terminal and Town linking with express service from Brockenhurst. Car ferries to Yarmouth. Bus services to all parts. Launching sites at public slipway adjacent yacht club, or at slipway at Town Quay. Car parks near. Yacht clubs: R. Lymington Y.C., Lymington Town S.C.

KEYHAVEN

Plan No. 22

Double High Water *at Hurst. First HW Springs* — *oo h. 55 m. Dover.*
Heights above Datum *MHWS 2m7. MLWS om5. MHWN 2m3. MLWN 1m3.*
Depths *On the bar om3 but liable to alter. Within the entrance between 3 and 4 m. About 1m5 off Mount Lake, then gradually decreasing to om2 at the quay.*

THE ENTRANCE to Keyhaven is exposed to easterly winds, but in normal conditions the river makes a very pleasant harbour for small craft. Unfortunately, it is so crowded by moorings that there is no room left for anchorage except near the entrance. The bar makes the entrance rather inconvenient if coming from the eastward, for if a yacht arrives on the last of the ebb she will have a longish wait for sufficient water to enter. If bound east from Keyhaven there is a similar wait for sufficient water over the bar.

Approach and Entrance Keyhaven lies on the north side of the Solent, 4 cables north-north-west of Hurst Point. If crossing the Solent allow for the strong athwartship tidal streams.

The entrance to Keyhaven Lake lies at 'North Point', the end of the shingle spit extending from Hurst Point. The point is conspicuous and stands out as a low sand and shingle promontory against a background of mud flats. There are two leading marks on the flats but they need not be followed exactly as there is no defined channel across the bar, which is fairly uniform with a depth of about om3; thus it can only be crossed with sufficient rise of tide.

Shape a course for a position about ¼ mile north-east of the old pier near Hurst High Light; then approach the entrance at about west-north-west with Yarmouth open astern. A small Sph BW buoy will be left to starboard at the entrance and course must be altered very sharply when (but not before)

52. *Rounding Hurst Point to Keyhaven. Tidal eddies in foreground, Hurst High Light, old pier, cottages and shingle shore extending towards river entrance on a misty morning.*

53. *Corner of Keyhaven Yacht Club and landing pontoon. To right hard and launching site and new quay.*

North Point comes abeam to leave its steep shingle extremity about 10m to port and the second of the series of Sph BW buoys to starboard. The channel at first bears to south-west and is at least 2m deep almost as far as Mount Lake; it is clearly marked by the starboard hand buoys in the first reach and round the bend to north-west as far as Mount Lake. Above that there are one or two port hand R buoys but the trend of the channel can be judged by the line of yachts on moorings in the centre, or farther upstream, where it is very shallow, by a double line of smaller craft.

Anchorage   The only anchorage in the Lake lies between North Point and the first of the private moorings which occupy the whole river farther up. There is a good anchorage in moderate westerly winds off the old pier near Hurst High

54. *Path from steps at Old Quay landing to Keyhaven Yacht Club.*

Light. To the north of it the water soon begins to shoal so that it becomes necessary to take soundings and anchor farther from the shore. On a summer Sunday many yachts anchor here with family parties who land and picnic on the Hurst beach. Close to the Old Pier the anchorage in Hurst Roads is tolerable even in strong south-west winds, but good ground tackle is needed in rough weather as there are strong tidal eddies.

Facilities Poor landing on steps at the end of Old Quay, better but little water at LWS at New Quay beyond the yacht club. Boat-builder for repairs and laying up. Hard for scrubbing with 1m8 at MHWS. Water and fuel from boatyard. Gun Inn, general stores, PO. EC Thurs. Very occasional buses. At Milford-on-Sea, 1 mile (1.6 km) distant, usual facilities of a small seaside town. EC Wed. Launching sites at Keyhaven hards with car park adjacent. Yacht clubs: Keyhaven Y.C., Hurst Castle S.C.

Plan No. 23

Double High Water *at entrance. First HW Springs — 02 h. 16 m. Dover, which is higher than the Second HW. Town Quay 25 m. later. HW at Neaps is variable, but Second HW is higher and may occur about +01 h. 00 m. Dover.*
Heights above Datum *(in harbour) MHWS 1m8. MLWS 0m4. MHWN 1m4. MLWN 0m6.*
Depths *About 0m4 on bar, but variable and may be lower in prolonged north and north-east winds. Off Mudeford Quay about 2m2. In the channel up to Christchurch there is considerable variation in depth—from 0m3 to 2m9.*

OWING to the shallow water over the bar 1m2 is about the maximum draught for entry at HW, except on exceptionally high tides or with local pilotage, which can be had by prior arrangement with Elkin's yacht yard. But once the difficulties of the entrance have been overcome, Christchurch harbour will be found an interesting place to visit. At Mudeford there is good bathing, and Christchurch itself is a beautiful old town, famous for the priory.

Approach and Entrance The entrance to Christchurch lies about a mile north of the conspicuous Hengistbury Head. The bar shifts frequently and varies in depth. Fresh onshore winds between south and east or heavy swell make the entrance dangerous, but in westerly winds some shelter is provided by Hengistbury Head which protects the entrance from the west.

There are two dangers when approaching from the west. Firstly the Christchurch ledges and secondly the Clarendon rocks off the shore on the south side of the entrance. From the

55. *The conspicuous white dome about ½ mile NE of Christchurch Bar.*

56. *Christchurch entrance and Haven Quay.*

north-east there are no outlying dangers, but on nearer approach frequent soundings should be taken to ensure an adequate depth of water.

The channel across the bar in 0m4 is not only very shallow but also very narrow and variable both in position and depths so a first visit to Christchurch should be made on a rising tide. The channel is marked by small Sph buoys, RW to port and B to starboard, but these occasionally drag after severe gales. If

57. *Christchurch Sailing Club, the Priory in centre, Elkin's yard and fuelling station on right.*

anchoring outside waiting rise of tide avoid anchoring on the rocky shoal shown on Plan No. 23. There are three landmarks which assist in finding the buoys: Haven House at the quay on the far side of the entrance bearing about west by south, a conspicuous big house near the beach among trees opposite the outer pair of buoys (at the time of writing), and a very conspicuous white dome on the shore about $\frac{1}{2}$ mile to the north east. Once the outer buoys have been identified, the channel may be entered. At the innermost RW buoy the channel bends sharply to port leaving the sea wall and the quay to starboard and the spit of submerged land to port. This channel is known as the 'Run', where there is the maximum rate of stream (reputed to attain 9 knots on an exceptional equinoxial spring ebb) and a depth of at least 2m1 at the quay.

Continuing up to Christchurch the channel is well marked by small Sph RW buoys to port and B to starboard. The streams are much weaker but at the time of writing the depth is lower to the east of Branders Bank (where it is marked 0m3 on the plan) than it is on the bar.

Moorings and Anchorage   As elsewhere, Christchurch harbour is occupied by moorings in all the best parts. Christchurch S.C. has two visitors' moorings and Elkin's yacht yard try to keep two deep-water moorings available. Yachts can anchor anywhere that room can be found but should keep clear of the centre of the buoyed channel as this is in frequent use, and avoid anchoring in the Run as the stream is fierce. Multi-hullers and twin-keelers which can dry out at LW have an advantage in harbours such as this.

Facilities   Three yacht or boat yards. Water, diesel and petrol at Elkin's jetty. Hotel, restaurants, banks, PO and many shops (EC Wed.) at Christchurch. Launching sites: (1) Slipway at Christchurch quay. (2) At sailing club, by permission. (3) At Elkin's yacht yard. (4) From beach on harbour side of Haven quay. Car parks adjacent. Yacht club: Christchurch S.C. Frequent buses and trains from Christchurch.

POOLE

Plan Nos. 24a and 24b. Admiralty Chart No. 2611

Double High Water *at entrance. First HW Springs −02 h. 36 m. Dover. At Poole Quay about 35 m. later. At Neaps the tides are weak and time of HW is almost unpredictable.*
Heights above Datum *Entrance MHWS 2m0. MLWS 0m3. MHWN 1m6. MLWN 1m1.*
Depths *3m7 on bar and in Main Channel to Poole Quay.*

POOLE HARBOUR is nearly 100 miles in circumference and the numerous channels provide interesting pilotage for small yachts. There are several privately-owned small islands, and in the centre is the comparatively large Brownsea Island, owned by the National Trust and well worth a visit. There is plenty of water for yachts of average size in the main channels, which are clearly marked, but the upper reaches of the various branches are uneven in depth and mostly shallow and a large scale chart is needed for their navigation. Range of tide is small but the streams at Springs are strong, especially in the entrance.

Approach and Entrance The prominent feature in the approach to Poole is the chalk Handfast Point, with Old Harry rocks off it. The bar buoy is situated a mile north-north-east of Handfast Point, and about 2 miles beyond the buoy will be seen the harbour entrance, with the conspicuous Haven Hotel on the east side.

There is an ugly sea on the bar and in the Swash entrance channel during strong winds between south and east, particularly on the ebb, when the approach may be dangerous. On the ebb there is a tide rip off Handfast Point.

The entrance channel, named the Swash, runs in at 322° from the Bar buoy to the Channel RW Cheq buoy between sands and a training bank on the west side, and the Hook Sand on the east side. The outer buoy is the Con B Bar light buoy and the channel is buoyed with RW can and barrel buoys (port)

58. *Poole. The chalk cliffs and Handfast Point, 1 mile south of Poole Bar Buoy, are conspicuous from a distance.*

59. *The beacon at the end of the training bank on west side of the Swash channel, and harbour entrance in background to right.*

and B Con buoys (starboard), but the buoys are close on the edge of the channel. There is a dolphin with light at the end of the training bank. At the Channel Light buoy (near the inner end of the training bank) alter course and steer for the entrance, leaving to starboard the Haven Hotel. A chain ferry crosses the entrance here. Care should be taken not to pass close ahead of the ferry when it is under way.

Inside the entrance the channel divides into two. One arm (South Deep) runs south-west, whilst the Main channel swings around between Sandbanks and Brownsea Island in a north-east direction and leads to Poole.

East Looe   This channel affords a short cut off Sandbanks from the eastward. Find the RY buoy at the entrance. Approach it at about 300°, or at night within the white sector of East Looe Shore Light, and leave it close to port. Then steer 245° to about ½ cable off the Haven Hotel where the East Looe joins the Swash channel. Leave the ends of the groynes to starboard and keep well north of the inner B Con (No. 19) Swashway buoy. Least water about 0m4 at the east end, but the sands are liable to alter.

The Harbour   The Main channel bears to north-north-east between North Haven Point beacon and the Middle Ground Sph No. 20 RW light buoy which is left to port. The channel is well marked by RW can buoys with even numbers to port and B Con buoys with odd numbers to starboard. The port hand buoys should not be passed closely. At Salterns pier after passing the marina the channel is narrow and the beacon should be left close to starboard. On arrival off Poole enter the Little or Stakes channel leaving No. 43 B Con Stakes buoy to starboard. Then leave the Hamworthy quay to port and three posts on the mud and a light beacon to starboard before altering course again to enter channel between quays.

In the other channels described below note that port hand stakes are painted red with red can topmarks; starboard hand stakes are black. Yellow stakes indicate oyster beds. When only one side of a channel is marked (such as those between the Wych and Main channels) the stakes are placed on the western side. Stakes at channel intersections are surmounted by a circle and have the names of the channel on boards below topmark.

The *Wych channel* lies on the north and north west sides of Brownsea Island, whence it pursues a wandering course between the mud flats to Shipstal Point and then southwards. It is deep and marked on the north side of the entrance by an intersection stake with a circular topmark and direction arms, one indicating the Wych channel and the other the Diver channel. It is then marked on each side by occasional piles on

60. *The east side of the entrance with conspicuous Sandbanks Hotel and block of flats. Brownsea Island to their left.*

the mud but the bed of the channel becomes uneven towards the west side of Brownsea Island, and especially where the channel bends from south to north-west. It then deepens for ¼ mile before shoaling gradually to only 0m1 off Shipstal Point on the Arne Peninsula.

The *Diver channel* lies between the Main channel and the Wych channel and it is the shortest way to Poole. Leave the Middle Ground Sph No. 20 buoy east of Brownsea Castle about ½ cable to starboard and steer for Salterns Bn true north. After opening up the Wych channel and the stakes which mark it, identify the intersection stake already referred to and the Aunt Betty RW Cheq light buoy No. 54 about 1½ cables north-west of it. Then steer to leave Aunt Betty and a stake close south-south-east of it to port to enter the Diver channel, which is marked by stakes and near its west end by the B Con Diver No. 49 light buoy where it joins the Main channel. The Diver channel carries 2m4 least water but at its entrance when approaching Aunt Betty 1m6 is crossed in the absence of local knowledge.

South Deep branches off to the south-west, west of North Haven Point, and is entered between No. 50A conical B buoy to starboard and No. 18 RW buoy to port, but do not round the port hand buoy sharply as there is a gravel bank in the vicinity. Steer south-west until the stakes are located—black to starboard, red to port. South Deep is not difficult to follow and it is deep as far as and ¼ mile beyond Goathorn Point. The channel lies between mud flats with beautiful heath land and distant hills to the south. There are no lights.

The upper reaches of the various channels are marked by stakes and are navigable, but great care is required in keel yachts as the bottom is very uneven. They are ideal for centreboard and light draught craft.

Lights By night the approach is easy. Make Poole Bar buoy (Qk Fl W Bell) and steer for the Channel buoy (Fl R 3 sec.) leaving the Training Bank beacon (Qk Fl R) well to port and the Hook Sand buoy (Fl W 3 sec.) opposite the Channel buoy to starboard. Then sail up the entrance towards Brownsea buoy (Qk Fl R) passing between the ferry hards (two F R H) on each side. Leave to starboard North Haven beacon (Fl W 5 sec.). Altering course here, refer to plan and proceed up the main channel between R Fl buoys to port and W Fl buoys to starboard. Salterns pier beacon (Gp Fl 3 W, 10 sec.) is

61. Brownsea Island and castle. North Haven beacon to right.

left close to starboard.

Anchorages and Berths (1) Outside. There is excellent holding ground in Studland Bay, protected from westerly and south-westerly winds. Small village with hotels, PO and grocer about ¼ mile inshore. EC Thurs. (2) Off Brownsea Island, but most of the area is occupied by private moorings. Hail the launchman for advice or enquire at the R. Motor Y.C. (who make visiting yachtsmen welcome) or at one of the yacht yards. (3) Moorings may sometimes be had inside the entrance on the east side in the North Haven Lake, off the yacht yard. Apply to boatman, yacht yard or yacht club. (4) Salterns Marina often has berths temporarily vacant. Dredged to 1m5 LAT (5) alongside the north quay in Poole town where other yachts are berthed west of the steps. (6) Cobb's Quay Marina in Holes Bay. All facilities, but ask at HM's office the times of opening bridge. Depths at marina about 1m2 MLWS, 1m8

MLWN, but soft bottom allows deeper draught. (7) Above Poole off the Dorset Lake Shipyard in Wareham channel, where there are sometimes moorings for hire, and attendance. (8) In west arm of harbour, i.e. in South Deep, as far up as and a cable beyond Goathorn Point.

Anchorage may be found anywhere in Poole harbour by choosing a position protected by land from the wind and free from moorings which are laid in all the best spots. In strong winds anchorage in open water areas may be uncomfortable for small craft, but shelter may be found at Poole Quay, or under a weather shore such as the Wych channel (protected from south by Brownsea Island) or off Goathorn Point (protection from west and south-west).

Facilities Yacht yards at Sandbanks, Parkstone and Hamworthy. Customs office. Water at tap or by hose on application at HM's office at Poole. Petrol at garages at bridge

62.   Poole Quay with yachts berthed to the left. (Photo : C. Sergel)

and quay where it is also available alongside in sealed cans or from yacht yards and marinas. Refueller moored in Diver channel near Aunt Betty buoy. Diesel fuel in bulk from road tankers at Town Quay by arrangement. Ship chandlers. Yacht brokers. Sailmakers. Hotels and many shops. EC Wed. Launching sites: Lilliput Yacht Service, Sandbanks Rd: end of quay farthest from Poole Bridge by arrangement with the crane hirers. Public launching slip at Baiter, east of Fishermans Dock. Yacht clubs: Lilliput S.C., R. Motor Y.C., Parkstone Y.C., Poole Harbour Y.C., Poole Y.C., Wareham S.C., Redcliffe S.C., East Dorset S.C., Converted Cruiser Club.

SWANAGE

In Settled weather and with winds between west-north-west and south-west there is a pleasant anchorage off the pier. When approaching care should be taken to avoid Peveril ledges off the south extremity of Swanage Bay. The tide sets strongly across the ledges. There is a RW Cheq buoy off the end of the ledges where there is a tidal race particularly on the south-south-west stream when the wind is contrary and it can be very rough. See Passage Notes.

The anchorage is a cable west-north-west of the end of the pier in about 2mo, seaward of local moorings, and larger yachts farther out, but the holding ground has weed in parts and is not so good as at Studland Bay, which has the additional advantage of Poole near at hand as a port of refuge in case of a change of wind or weather. Lt F R at end of pier.

Excellent hotels and shopping facilities. EC Thurs. Good sailing club (Swanage S.C.) which welcomes holiday membership. Launching site at slipway near pier with car park adjacent. Buses.

63. *Conspicuous hotel left, pier centre, yachts at anchor on right.*

64.   Lulworth Cove. Enter east of midway in the entrance. (Photo : Aerofilms Ltd.)

LULWORTH COVE

Plan No. 25

High Water *approx.* −04 h. 49 m. *Dover.*
Heights above Datum *MHWS 2m1. MLWS 0m2. MHWN 1m4. MLWN 0m7.*
Depths *About 5m0 in entrance; 3m0 in centre, shallows towards shore.*

LULWORTH should only be visited in settled weather and during offshore winds. A shift of wind to south or south-west, bringing with it a strong blow as so frequently happens, will send a heavy swell into the cove. In such conditions power vessels may find it difficult to get out in safety and the task of beating out under sail may prove too dangerous to attempt. Therefore, clear out if the weather threatens to change and if caught inside, apply to local boatmen for heavy anchors and cables.

Lulworth Cove is in a lovely setting and is worth altering course to visit. There are good coastal walks to the westward but east of the cove there are gunnery ranges. Red flags are flown when firing is in progress.

Lulworth Gunnery Ranges There are two danger areas for shipping to the south of Lulworth and Kimmeridge. The inner one extends 14 km out to sea and the outer, which is seldom used, extends out to 22 km. Times of firing are published in local papers and notified to neighbouring HM

65. *Entering Lulworth Cove from seaward. The white road is conspicuous when coming from eastward and the ex-coastguard hut on the summit of the west headland can just be seen.*

and yacht clubs. They can also be obtained from the Range Office, telephone Bindon Abbey 462721 ext. 259. When firing is in progress red flags are flown by day and lights flashing red shown at night, at the summit of Bindon Hill and on St Alban's Head. Vessels may pass through the areas but passage must be made as quickly as possible and anchorage, fishing or stopping is prohibited. When the range is active fast range patrol boats are on station for safety reasons and to advise yachtsmen of the extent of the area.

Approach and Entrance   Lulworth is not always easy to identify from seaward, but the photograph reproduced will help. To the west there runs a series of white cliffs with curved summits. The entrance is just to the east of a sugar-loaf hill with an ex-coastguard hut situated upon it.

There are rocks on both sides of the entrance of the cove but those on the west extend farther than those on the east, so keep east of the centre. Once past these rocks the fairway opens into the wide cove itself.

As may be expected, the wind is fluky or squally at the entrance, and frequently baffling when entering under sail.

Anchorage   No anchorage outside. Let go anchor in about 2m4 on the north side of the cove where the holding ground is blue clay or on north-west in south-west winds. Avoid anchoring in the fairway to the beach landing of Lulworth village on the north-west side of cove.

Facilities   Water at tap in car park or beach café may oblige. Petrol and oil at garage. Small hotels. PO. Shops, EC Wed Sat. Launching site from beach at end of road, with car park adjacent. Provisions at Boon's stores during summer months. Frequent buses in summer months.

WEYMOUTH

Plan No. 26

High Water   *− 04 h. 38 m. Dover.*
Heights above Datum   *MHWS 2m1. MLWS 0m2. MHWN 1m4. MLWN 0m7.*
Tides   *The tides are 4 hours flood, 4 hours ebb, and 4 slack subject to the 'Gulder' as it is called, which is a small flood with a rise of approx. 0m2 making its way into the harbour about ¾ hr. after the first LW.*
Depths   *The entrance and north side where ships berth is dredged to 4m6. There is less water on the south side.*

WEYMOUTH, as popular seaside resorts go, is a pleasant one. The town provides most facilities for yachtsmen, and there is a good train service to London via Dorchester, Poole and Southampton. The harbour is sheltered but in strong easterly winds the approach can be rough and there is sometimes an uncomfortable swell in the area of the pier heads.

Approach and Entrance   The harbour lies about ½ mile north of the Portland Harbour breakwaters. The entrance is between two piers. On the south is the Nothe Hill, and on the north pier is the Pavilion. The Jubilee Clock—conspicuous—is about ½ mile north along the front. Approaching from the eastward several buoys will be seen—see chart—and will be left well to port. Three of these are light buoys; the outer two are the D.G. Range buoys Bl W (Fl W 5 sec.) and Bl W (Qk Fl R), the inner buoy which lies off the Mixen rocks, marking the sewer outfall, is BY (Fl R). Then steer a cable off the entrance and round in between the two piers. There are two white triangular leading marks at 237½° on the south quay for ships

66. *Entering Weymouth harbour. South pier and light with Nothe in background.*

but they need not be followed by yachts. Keep clear of the fairway in the lower part of the harbour when there are hauling-off ropes across the harbour and a Cross Channel Ferry Steamer is about to depart.

Regulating Signals From north pier a red flag over a green by day, or two red lights over a green at night indicate entry or departure forbidden. Two red flags by day or three red lights by night indicate a vessel is leaving and no vessel shall approach or obstruct the entrance. Two green flags by day or three green lights by night indicate that a vessel is approaching entrance from seaward and no vessel may leave. When no signal is shown the entrance is clear, both inwards and outwards. Within the harbour limits boats, whether under

oars, sails or power, are to keep clear of the main channel, and not to obstruct or impede the passage of vessels entering or leaving.

Lights and Fog Signals North pier, F G. South pier, Qk Fl W 10m 9M (obscured over Mixen rocks). Two F R leading lights on south side of harbour in line at 237½° lead in, open of the south pier light. Fog signals: South pier explosives (3) Reed ev 15 sec. when vessel expected. North pier, bell.

Anchorage Visiting yachts during daylight should close the Pier Master's office on the starboard hand at entrance and will usually be directed to a berth in the Cove. If the Pier Master's office is not manned or if there is a heavy swell go right up the harbour and moor alongside the Cove Quay on the

67. *Within the entrance. White triangle leading marks are for ships which berth on north side.*

port side about a cable short of the bridge. This is the most popular berth for small yachts and is often crowded by yachts lying abreast. Anchorage outside the harbour may be found in settled weather and offshore winds in 2 to 3m about a cable north-west of the end of the pier, clear of the entrance and the turning space required by Channel Island ferries. Take soundings to find right depth, as shallow water extends a long way seaward. The depths of water alongside the Cove Quay

68. The Cove to which small yachts are usually directed and where they lie abreast.

wall vary from 0m1 to 0m4 at LAT, but a pontoon is usually positioned at the shallowest part. At a distance of 3m from the quay there is 1m0 increasing to 4m towards mid-channel.

Facilities Yacht yards and chandlers. Customs Office. Water at Cove and at quays. Fuel at quayside, by arrangement. Hotels, restaurants and shops. EC Wed. Station and buses. Launching sites from slipway in harbour by prior permission of HM or at yards. Yacht clubs: R. Dorset Y.C., Weymouth S.C.

PORTLAND

Plan No. 27

High Water *− 04 h. 38 m. Dover.*
Heights above Datum *MHWS 2m1. MLWS 0m2.*
MHWN 1m4. MLWN 0m7.
Depths *Deep ship harbour except on its western side.*

PORTLAND HARBOUR lies in the bay formed by the mainland on the north, the long narrow strip of the Chesil Beach on the west, and the high peninsula of Portland on the south. From the east it is protected by three big breakwaters which create a very large artificial harbour. This is primarily a naval base but it also provides shelter for yachts, though it can be rough in gales.

Strangers should remember that it is a naval port. Within the harbour there are numerous unlit floating targets, mooring buoys, etc., and cables on bottom. Attention is also drawn to the increasing number of naval exercises being carried out from Portland and in the adjacent waters with both submarine and surface craft. Also night exercises often involve flares, Very lights and flashes, etc.

Approach and Entrance Portland is so conspicuous that it is easy to identify. It is a high peninsula that, viewed from seaward, resembles an island, but the highest part is at the northern end, and the southern extremity (the Bill) is low.

The principal danger to navigation in the approach to Portland is the Race. This is the most dangerous disturbance on the whole of the south coast, and the time of tide has to be studied—see Passage Notes.

The harbour itself may be located behind its long stone breakwaters, northward of the heights of Portland. There were three entrances, but the South Ship channel has been closed. The two entrances in use are the East and North Ship channels.

Principal Lights and Fog Signals Portland Bill lighthouse: Gp Fl W 20 sec. 43m. 29M. Gradually changes one Fl to four Fl from 221° to 244°, four Fl 244° to 117° (which is the principal sector), gradually changes to one Fl thence to 141°, obscured elsewhere. F R Lt below visible over Shambles 271° to 291°. Diaphone 30 sec. *South-west end of outer breakwater:* Occ R 30 sec. 5M obscured seaward. *East Ship Channel:* 'A' Head Fl W 10 sec. 22m 20M (north side); Fort Head inconspicuous F R 2M (south side). *North Ship channel:* 'C' Head Occ W 10 sec. 11m 5M (north side); 'B' Head Occ R 15 sec. 11m 5M (south side).

Regulations No vessel may exceed 12 knots without licence from Queen's HM. Yachts should not approach H.M. ships or jetties closely.

Sailing vessels and power-driven vessels of less than 20m length shall not hamper the safe passage of large power-driven vessels which are entering and leaving the channels between the breakwaters, or are under way within the limits of the harbour.

Anchorage There is anchorage off Old Castle Cove in the north-west of the harbour, with depths of 2 to 3m. Yachts should anchor outside the yachts on private moorings of which there are a great number. It is better if possible to get use of a vacant mooring. Inquire of the boatman or the Castle Cove S.C. Visiting yachtsmen are usually permitted to use the landing-stage belonging to the sailing club. There is water from a tap on the shore. PO, shops and town are ¼ mile (0.4 km) distant. To Weymouth is a walk of over ½ mile (0.8 km) or alternatively go by bus.

In strong southerly and south-west winds this anchorage is

69. *Portland Bill and beacon from the SW, where it should be given a berth of at least 100 metres at LW. See also Passage Notes, Part II.*

too exposed. In this case bring up in the anchorage to the west of the R.3. Hard, ½ mile west of Castletown which is sheltered by the Chesil Beach and land from west and south winds, but even so can be very rough during gales owing to wind eddies.

Yachtsmen are allowed to land on the R.N.S.A. (Portland Branch) pontoons close to the castle and inquiry can be made for possible use of a mooring here. Castletown pier is private, and there is no public landing except on the beach just east of

70. *Castletown Beach, the only public landing place on the south side of Portland Harbour other than the RNSA pontoons.*

it. To the north and west of the pier there is a helicopter landing approach area: note the Prohibited Anchorage shown on the harbour plan.

Facilities At Castletown. Water obtainable from Royal Breakwater Hotel or public houses. Fuel from garages at Victoria Sq. ¼ mile (0.4 km) distant. PO and shops. EC Wed. Grocers Sat. Banks and wider range of shops at Fortuneswell, ½ mile distant. Yacht yards at Ferrybridge. Launching site: rather restricted but light boats can be launched from Castletown beach, road adjacent, or from beach adjacent to bridge at Wyke Regis which joins mainland to Chesil causeway. Yacht clubs: Castle Cove S.C., R.N.S.A. (Portland Branch).

BRIDPORT

Plan No. 28

High Water — *05 h. 11 m. Dover.*

Heights above Datum *In approach approx. MHWS 4 m1. MLWS 0m6. MHWN 3m0. MLWN 1m6.*

Depths *Bar within entrance between piers dries out. From 0m6 to 1m5 within harbour, one deep berth, but most parts dry out, except for the coaster berths and their turning area.*

WESTBAY, which is the port of Bridport, suffers from the usual disadvantage of a shallow artificial harbour which has a long narrow entrance. The entrance is dangerous in hard onshore weather. Once inside the harbour a yacht may be weather bound waiting for fair conditions before attempting to leave, but this old West Country port is worth a visit, and offers a pleasant break to the passage across West Bay. There is a coaster trade with the import of timber and export of shingle. Near LWS the sluice gates are opened and the entrance is scoured with the water released.

Approach and Entrance The approach to Bridport harbour is simple enough so far as outlying dangers are

71. Bridport (West Bay) entrance from south. (Photo: P. E. Payne)

103

72. *The harbour. Coaster berth on right.*

concerned, but the harbour entrance is unsafe in strong onshore winds, as the sea breaks heavily outside even at high water.

When a vessel is expected and when there is sufficient depth a pilot flag is hoisted on the east pier flagstaff; when the entrance is considered unsafe a black ball is hoisted. The presence of these signals should not be relied upon for yachts, as they are hoisted for ships.

The only outlying shoals are the Pollock, 4m3, to the south-west, and the High Ground, 3m1, to the west. From the west to steer between these shoals bring North Hill on east side of harbour in line with east pier at 075° true.

From south or east, steer straight off the entrance and, with sufficient rise of tide, enter but beware of the backwash off the piers. The recognized line of approach is West Pierhead and Bridport Church tower in line at 011°. The bar lies within the entrance and dries out but carries 3m or more at MHWS. The channel is long and narrow (12m) and sailing craft without auxiliaries will need to be towed in during offshore winds.

Lights The entrance should not be attempted by strangers at night. A Lt Iso W 1½ sec. 9m 5M is established on HM's office on foreshore just west of west pier, but this serves only as a guide to the position of the harbour. When a vessel is expected pilot lights are exhibited: F G on east pierhead and F

73. *At low water most of the harbour dries out except from the sluice to the coaster berth.*

R on west pierhead, range 2M.

Anchorages and Moorings (1) Outside the harbour in settled weather with offshore winds. Anchor about cable off the entrance in 2m4 clear of leading lines and sewer or seaward in deeper water. (2) Inside the harbour consult the HM. Small yachts dry out at the west end of the harbour, or alongside the harbour walls. There are coaster berths (3m3) alongside northern end of the east quay where scour from sluice makes a deep hole. Apply to the HM for the use of one, which he permits when no coaster is expected. Otherwise berth at east end of harbour drying alongside quay, soft mud bottom.

Facilities Water from hydrants near the quay. Diesel and petrol at local garage. Shops and stores. EC Thurs. Scrubbing inside harbour; no yacht yard. Launching site: good slip and adjacent car park. Good bus connections.

LYME REGIS

Plan No. 29

High Water − 04 h. 53 m. Dover.
Heights above Datum *in approach approx. MHWS 4m3.
MLWS om6. MHWN 3m1. MLWN 1m7.*
Depths *about 1mo a cable east of the entrance, more to
seaward. Harbour dries out at LW and entrance is less than 1mo.*

LYME REGIS and its harbour are picturesque and worth visiting, though crowded in the holiday season. The harbour dries out but a berth alongside the quay is sheltered from northerly, westerly and south-west winds and in these winds the harbour is said to be safe even in gales. In strong onshore winds the approach is very rough and in south-east gales the approach and entrance are dangerous; the swell enters the harbour.

Approach and Entrance Lyme Regis is just east of the centre of Lyme Bay, some 22 miles west of Portland Bill. The approach is straightforward. The harbour is protected from the west by the long stone pier known as 'The Cobb', which is forked at its eastern end. At the end of the outer fork is a beacon off which there is a post marking a heap of large Portland stones, serving as a breakwater and covered at half flood. There are also stones and rocks all along the west and south of the Cobb.

The entrance to the harbour lies between the eastern end of

74. *Lyme Regis. Approach from south showing the Cobb, breakwater and rocks marked by a post at their extremity.*

75. *Entrance of Lyme Regis harbour from the eastward.*

76. *Lyme Regis quay where there are berths for visiting yachts opposite the sailing club.*

the inner fork of the Cobb and the southern end of the detached breakwater which affords partial protection to the harbour from the east. The entrance is narrow.

Steer for the beacon off the outer fork of the Cobb, leaving the post off it about 50m to port and hold on until the harbour entrance is opened up. Then steer in, given sufficient rise of tide, to enter the harbour.

Leading Lights   Front light on inner pierhead F W R 2M. Rear light on old lamp-post F R 2M. Lights in line lead in at 296°. The lights are weak and on approach are rendered inconspicuous by the many town lights ashore.

Anchorages and Moorings   (1) Anchor outside the harbour in settled weather and offshore winds to the east of the entrance. The anchor symbol on the plan shows the most northerly position in about 1mo LAT, as the water shoals rapidly towards the shore. It is better to anchor in deeper water further seaward if remaining for any length of time, especially at spring tides, but less protection from the west. Take soundings to find the right depth, but it is better to consult the HM as the quality of the bottom varies. (2) Most of the harbour dries out and the moorings in the centre are for permanently moored boats. At the quay opposite the sailing club house there are mooring berths for twelve visiting yachts only, but it is advisable to contact the HM in advance to reserve a berth. The inmost berth dries about 1m3 at LAT on clean sand bottom and the outer 0m3.

Facilities   Water at shoreward end of the Cobb. Fuel delivered for small fee. Hotels and shops. EC Thurs. Scrubbing can be arranged and small yacht repairs. Launching site, slip and car park adjacent. Dinghy park. Buses to all parts. Nearest station Axminster 6 miles (9.6 km) Yacht club: Lyme Regis S.C.

BEER

IN NORTHERLY winds and settled weather there is a delightful anchorage for small yachts off Beer. This is sheltered from the north to west by Beer Head. Beer Head is a precipitous headland, 130m high, and easy to identify, as it is the most westerly chalk cliff in England. The anchorage is on the west side of the small bay east of Beer Head, as close to the shore as soundings show desirable. Approaching from the westward, round Beer Head and follow up the cliffs (which have rocks at their base) keeping on the west side towards the conspicuous road which leads from the shore to the village and church. Approaching from the eastward give a wide berth to the headland on the east side of the cove, which has rocks extending over a cable off it, before turning into the anchorage. Land by dinghy on beach which is steep. There are local fishermen and boatmen who will ferry to the yacht or attend to the dinghy.

With any forecast of change in wind leave quickly. The local fishing boats are hauled up on the beach out of danger. For yachts the nearest good harbour of refuge is Brixham.

Facilities   Hotels, shops. EC Thurs. Boat-builder. Launching site from the road leading down to the beach which is steep and suitable for launching.

77. *Rounding Beer Head from the westward.*

78. *Beer Bay and anchorage. Author's former yacht to right.*

Plan No. 30

High Water *Exmouth Dock. −04 h. 53 m. Dover. At Topsham ½ h. later.*
Heights above Datum *Approaches MHWS 4m5. MLWS 0m5. MHWN 3m3. MLWN 1m7. Dock about 0m5 less.*
Depths *The approach and sands are liable to change, and the buoys are moved to conform. Plan No. 30 is based on the new issue Admiralty Chart No. 2290 corrected from Notices to Mariners issued in 1975 but the sands frequently change. The depth of the bar is about 1m5 (2m0 MLWS). Within the harbour the bottom is uneven. There are deep stretches off Exmouth town and south and south-west of Bull Hill Bank but on the west and north of the bank there are 1m5 patches. The river tends to shoal towards Topsham and practically dries out in the upper reaches.*

THE RIVER EXE provides some 6 miles of navigable channel. It is worth visiting when cruising in the West Country. The only harbour is a small tidal dock at Exmouth town but there are several anchorages. It should not be regarded as a port of refuge as the sands on the bar are liable to shift and there is a dangerous sea during strong onshore winds, especially with the ebb running against the wind. Under average conditions, however, the approach and entrance are not difficult being well buoyed.
Approach and Entrance The outer Fairway buoy (Sph bell buoy RW Vert bands) is situated ½ mile south-south-west of Straight Point, which is a low promontory backed by red cliffs, but should not be confused with the lower Orcombe Point a mile westward. There are high cliffs between the two

79. *Exmouth fairway buoy.*

with ledges of rock at their foot. Whatever the direction of the approach, make for the Fairway buoy but when coming from the direction of Torbay or Teignmouth give a good offing to the Pole sands on the south side of the entrance channel, which are extending eastwards.

As stated, the entrance should not be attempted during strong onshore winds especially if the ebb has started to run. The easiest time to approach is half flood. This coincides with the turn of the offshore stream to the west. The tidal streams in the offing are weak but are very strong in the channel and the entrance. As the sands are liable to shift after gales it is necessary to navigate up the channel by the buoys (which are moved accordingly), leaving the even-numbered R and RW can buoys to port and the odd-numbered B Con buoys to starboard. Some of the port hand buoys are very close to the Pole sands so they should not be approached too closely. The streams run like torrents after the last port buoy (No. 10) has been passed and it is best then to keep on the starboard side of the fairway.

The River   Off Exmouth the river takes a sharp turn to the south-west between Bull Hill Bank in the middle of the harbour and the Warren sands which form a continuation of the Warren (the low point on the south side of the entrance). The main flood sweeps past Exmouth in a north-westerly direction and accordingly course should be altered sharply to port well before reaching the dock in order to get into the stream between Bull Hill Bank and the Warren sands, and in particular to avoid the shoals extending easterly from Bull Hill Bank. The reach of the river south of the Bull Hill Bank is called the Bight and is marked by two starboard hand buoys and by mooring buoys on the port hand. The channel follows round Bull Hill Bank northward and bends, leaving the RW Cheq spit buoy and the Shaggles sand to port and No. 17 buoy close to starboard. Course (see Imray Laurie Norrie &

Wilson Chart Y No. 45) should then be towards the Lympstone Church to the north-north-east, passing between No. 12 RW port hand and No. 19 B starboard buoys. The channel then bears in a north-north-west direction towards Powderham, leaving to starboard No. 21, No. 23 B buoys and perch, soon bearing north-north-east again leaving to port Powderham Pool and No. 14 RW buoy. Then follow the buoys in a shoaling channel with depths as low as 1m5 in parts nearly to Turf Lock. Above Turf Lock the channel is marked by beacons on either side as far as Topsham.

When proceeding from Exmouth up the river a considerable saving of distance can be made by passing through the Shelly Gut. This is a shallow channel on the east side of Bull Hill Bank but it can only be used with local knowledge as the sands are steep-to on either side and the channel is intricate.

The Starcross channel lies west of the Shaggles sand and carries 0m9 to 2m1 as far as Starcross. It is entered at the Shaggles Spit RW Cheq buoy (leaving it to starboard). Although the channel is unmarked except by a beacon on the port side, the best water can be located by the larger yachts lying on moorings in it.

The Western Way   This is a drying swashway between the Pole sands on the eastward side and the Warren sands on the western side. It requires local knowledge and a shallow draught boat.

Lights   Straight Point Lt Fl W R 10 sec. 34m 9M and 7M W 246°–012½°; R to 022½°; W to 017°.

The approach is marked by Fl or Qk Fl W Lts on the starboard hand (which is the easier side to follow) and by Lts on two buoys (Qk Fl R and Fl R 3 sec.) on the port hand. There are two Lts, F Or 7M, near the Custom House and the dock which lead in line at 305°; but the transit crosses the outer end of the Pole sands and is only of service from No. 6 port hand buoy (no light) to the Checkstone No. 10 port hand buoy Fl R

80. *View from No. 7 buoy heading seawards approximately ESE, with Orcombe Point in centre and Straight Point beyond.*

3 sec. Within the harbour there are the starboard hand light buoys as shown on Plan No. 30.

Anchorage and Moorings (1) Temporary anchorage outside off the entrance west of the Fairway buoy in calm weather. (2) Exmouth dock. This is approached through a narrow entrance where ferries berth, and is spanned by a narrow bridge which has to be opened by arrangement with the HM. The basin is tidal and the north-west side dries out and is occupied by boats. HM's office is on south side of the bridge and with his permission yachts berth at the south-east quays if these are not occupied by coasters. Depths about 1m2 alongside quay but less water in centre. Keel yachts will partially dry and there are a few ladders. When entering allow for the very strong streams setting across the entrance. (3) Anchor (if room can be found clear of moorings) beyond the entrance to the dock off the Point in 3m, clear of the lifeboat. Five-knot tidal stream at spring tides and rough when a fresh wind against stream. (4) Large yachts may anchor clear of the fairway in the Bight between Bull Hill Bank and Warren sands. (5) West of Bull Hill Bank outside the small craft moorings. (6) Anchorage off Starcross, south-east of the pier in 0m6 to 2m1 but best positions occupied by private moorings. Enquire at club as to possible temporary vacancy. Well sheltered from west. Water, and some facilities. EC Thurs. Ferry to

81. View after passing No. 10 buoy and heading towards the dock with Exmouth seafront on right.

Exmouth. Main line station. (7) There is a mooring area between the perch, No. 25 buoy and Lympstone sand which is approached from No. 23 buoy and stated to have an approximate depth of 1m0 at LW. (8) Small craft can anchor in 1m5 south of landing stage at Turf, clear of the coasters fairway, or north of No. 25 buoy.

Exeter Canal The canal is 5 miles (8 km) long and is entered at Turf Lock. Least depth 3m3. Locked basin at Exeter.

Facilities at Exmouth. Boat-builders and repairers. Cus-toms. Water by hose at dock. Petrol and oil. Hotels and shops. EC Wed. Launching sites: (1) Ramp south of harbour entrance near HW, where yacht club puts a wooden ramp over the soft sand in summer months, little room in road for cars and trailers but car park on the pier. (2) Beach north of harbour entrance. (3) By arrangement with yacht yards. (4) At Lympstone, 2 miles north of Exmouth ramp for launching near HW. Yacht clubs: Exe S.C., Starcross Y.C. at Pow-derham Pt, Starcross Fishing and Cruising Club at Starcross, Topsham S.C., Lympstone S.C. Station and bus services.

TEIGNMOUTH

Plan No. 31

High Water *approaches* −*05 h. 11 m. Dover.*
Heights above Datum *MHWS 4m8. MLWS 0m6.
MHWN 3m6. MLWN 1m9.*
Depths *About 0m3 on the bar ; deep pool off Ferry Point,
then depths over 2m nearly to Shaldon bridge.*

TEIGNMOUTH is an attractive little seaside town. The
harbour on its west and south-west side is well sheltered but
the streams are fast so that it is best to obtain moorings if
possible. The entrance is difficult for strangers and the bar
makes it dangerous during onshore winds and when a swell is
running.

Approach and Entrance The entrance to the River
Teign lies to the northward of the Ness, a bold red sandstone
headland with pines at its summit which is easy to identify.
The Ness and the Pole sands projecting eastward from it flank
the south side of the river entrance, and the Spratt sands lie on
the north side. The sands on the bar are constantly shifting and
in some years steep sandbanks build up. Without a pilot or
assistance from local fishermen or boat-owners the entrance
should not be attempted by strangers, except with the utmost
caution in settled weather during offshore winds and on the
last quarter of the flood. The following sailing directions form
a rough guide to the entrance but should not be relied upon as
there are no clear leading marks owing to the shifting sands.

Approach from the southward with the *inner* end of the pier
bearing about north magnetic. When the Ness comes abeam a
small black buoy, maintained by the pilots, will be seen. This is
usually moored on the west side of the East Pole sand and (if in
position) is left close on the starboard hand. Here there is

82.   The Ness (red sandstone) and to right the white beacon.

83.   Close up of the conspicuous white light beacon.

usually about 0m3.

To the west will be seen a white beacon on the north-west side of the Ness, on a training wall which is covered before half flood. When this beacon bears between 250° and 258° steer about 40m off it, taking soundings to skirt the north side of the Pole sands. An alternative and more direct approach is from the east to make a position with the white beacon (which is conspicuous) bearing 254°, distant 4 cables and proceed as before. In either case it is sensible in tidal calculations to assume that an area drying 0m6 will be crossed, as a stranger may not find the best water and the sands are liable to change.

On arrival off this beacon steer by chart round the black

84. In the reach east of The Salty with New Quay on left and Yacht Yard on starboard hand, off which there is a visitors' mooring.

starboard hand buoy off Ferry Point on the north side of the channel. Note that the sands have crept southwards from the point so the buoy should not be approached too closely. Here the stream runs very hard. Once past Ferry Point alter course quickly to starboard at 021° and steer for the end of the New Quay leaving three red can buoys well to port.

The whole of the centre of the harbour is occupied by 'The Salty' flat and the river runs on the east of this. Pilotage is easier because the flats are marked by port hand cask buoys. To starboard the shore is fairly steep. After passing the third red port hand buoy keep on the starboard side of the channel on the line of New Quay until rounding into the straight reach, north of the Salty, leading to the bridge. Here the direction of the channel can be judged by yachts lying on moorings, keeping close to the larger ones for the best water.

Lights　There will be an identification light Fl RW on the south-east side of the Ness but strangers should not attempt the entrance at night, as the leading lights are intended for the assistance of pilots who have local knowledge.

Anchorage and Mooring　Anchoring is possible outside Teignmouth harbour 1 to 2 cables south-east of the pier end or a cable south-east of the Ness in settled weather and offshore winds, taking soundings to find a suitable depth. Within the harbour it is difficult to anchor as the streams are strong and there are moorings and chains on the bottom in all the best parts. The only possibility is at Neap tides on the edge of The Salty near the second and third red buoys. Accordingly it is necessary to try to find a vacant mooring. There is a visitors' mooring off the yacht yard on the east side of the channel in deep water. Moor fore and aft to two white buoys with a 15m spread. Enquiry can also be made of the HM at New Quay as to the possibility of a mooring being temporarily vacant.

Upper Reaches　(Y Chart No. 46)　The river above Shaldon bridge is navigable as far as Newton Abbot at high water by small craft with local knowledge.

Facilities　Water from New Quay. Fuel and chandlery but Shaldon better for this purpose. Yacht yard with patent slipway up to 36m and 2m7 draught, and two small boat yards. Several hotels and restaurants. Good shops. EC Thurs. Launching site for dinghies at Shaldon. At Teignmouth launching is possible at the end of Lifeboat Lane and Gales Hill, also at Pellew Steps, and there is a launching site at the yacht yard. Ferry from Ferry Point to Shaldon. Yacht clubs: Teign Corinthian Y.C., Shaldon S.C. Buses and mainline station.

116

TORQUAY

Plan No. 32

High Water −05 h. 08 m. Dover.

Heights above Datum *MHWS 4m9. MLWS 0m7. MHWN 3m7. MLWN 2m0.*

Depths *4m2 just within the entrance. Inside the outer harbour there is over 3m alongside the Haldon (east) pier, and the Princess (west) pier. In the southern part of the harbour the depth is over 2m, but the inner harbour dries out except at the end of the south pier.*

TORQUAY lies in the north-western corner of Torbay. The harbour is convenient and is sheltered, except in onshore winds, which, if strong, can make conditions inside uncomfortable. The town is a large and popular seaside resort and hence crowded during the holiday season.

Approach and Entrance Approaching from the eastward the church tower on high ground at the back of Babbacombe Bay and the spire of the Roman Catholic church will first be seen. Torbay will next be identified with Hope Nose and the Ore Stone (32m) and Thatcher (41m) rocks on the north side and Berry Head on the south. Entering the north side of the bay note that there is a sunken outlier about 90m south-west of Ore Stone, and the Morris Rogue (0m8 over it) 1½ cables south-east of the East Shag (11m) rock.

85.   *The Ore Stone (outer) and Thatcher rocks are conspicuous on the northern extremity of Torbay. The picture faces north.*

86. *Torquay harbour and entrance showing Princess pier (left), Haldon pier (right) and south pier of the inner drying harbour. Moorings for yachts are shown and also the dinghy slips in outer harbour and the slip in the inner harbour. (Photo : Aerofilms Ltd.)*

From the southward there are no outlying dangers. The entrance is 61m wide, and within the outer harbour there is plenty of water for yachts. There is not much room for manœuvre, so enter slowly, or under reduced sail, and be prepared to meet excursion vessels, which are frequently leaving the harbour.

Lights South of the entrance a buoy Qk Fl W (April/Sept.). On the Haldon (east) pierhead a Lt F G (W over harbour); on Princess (west) pierhead a Lt F R (W over harbour). On the inner pier there is a Lt F W.

Anchorage and Moorings (1) Outside, in offshore winds, good anchorage off the Princess pier in 3m6 to 4m8 or near the end of the Haldon pier in 2m4 to 2m7 or more to seaward but keep clear of the fairway. (2) Inside harbour. Moor to buoy as directed by the HM, or berth temporarily alongside Haldon Pier. Large yachts lie inside to east and west of entrance, smaller ones farther in. The outer piers are in constant use by pleasure and excursion vessels in summer months, but yachts sometimes lie alongside the wall in inner harbour and dry out.

Facilities Water from tap near dinghy landing on east of outer harbour or in quantity at the Haldon pier or the south pier. Petrol, diesel oil and chandlery at south pier. Boat-builders. Scrubbing by arrangement. Launching site at all states of tide on slip on east of outer harbour with car park adjacent (often full); also at slipway in inner harbour, 3 hours each side of HW, by permission of the HM. Hotels and restaurants of all grades. Excellent shops. EC Wed. or Sat. Main-line station. Buses to all parts and coaches. Ferry to Brixham. Yacht club: R. Torbay Y.C.

PAIGNTON

PAIGNTON HARBOUR lies on the west side of Torbay north of Roundham Head, which is a prominent red cliff headland. There is a rock spit running eastward from the east quay, the seaward extremity of which is marked by a lattice beacon with a spoil ground topmark. Approach from north-east is simplest.

The harbour dries out and is crowded with moorings but there is good anchorage in offshore winds north-east of the entrance within easy reach of the harbour by dinghy. Facilities are good and the HM can sometimes arrange a berth where a visiting yacht can dry out alongside the quay.

BRIXHAM

Plan No. 33

High Water −05 h. 11 m. Dover.
Heights above Datum *MHWS 4m7. MLWS 0m7.
MHWN 3m4. MLWN 1m9.*
Depths *The outer harbour is deep but the inner harbour dries out at Springs almost to the end of the New pier.*

BRIXHAM is an historic fishing port, and the whole harbour used to be occupied by sailing trawlers and their moorings. Sail has been replaced by motor trawlers but the industry is active and prosperous, as the innumerable sea gulls bear witness. The big outer harbour is available for yachts and is easily accessible at all states of the tide, which makes it one of the best yachting centres in the West Country. The Brixham Yacht Club is the centre of sailing activity, and hospitable to visiting yachtsmen of recognized clubs. The outer harbour is sheltered except from the northward and Torbay provides a fine sailing area with weak tides which is open only to the eastward.

87.   *Mooring area. Brixham Yacht Club landing and stacked inflatable dinghies centre of background.*

88.   *View of Brixham Harbour facing NW towards Torquay.* From left *the inner harbour and breakwater. The new pier and fish market with Brixham Yacht Club behind it and the principal mooring area.*

Approach and Entrance Brixham lies a mile west of Berry Head, which is a headland, sloping at 45°, easily identified. The harbour entrance is wide but the end of the breakwater should not be rounded closely when approaching from east as trawlers and Torbay excursion ferries may be leaving the harbour and hidden by the breakwater. Speed limit within is 5 knots.

Lights Berry Head Lt, Gp Fl (2) W 15 sec. 58m 18M. At end of breakwater Lt Occ R 15 sec. 3M. For lights inside the harbour see the plan.

Anchorages (1) Outside in Brixham Roads in about 7m, or small yachts can find anchorage in fine weather outside in the corner formed between the inner end of the breakwater and the cliffs extending towards Berry Head, sheltered from west to south. (2) Inside on west side of the harbour as indicated on the plan, between moorings and just clear of fairway. Inevitably there is often considerable wash from passing trawlers and excursion boats if near the fairway, so close to the land near the entrance is preferable in reasonable weather. (3) Small yachts can anchor in Fishcombe Cove (just west of the headland at entrance) but this position can be dangerous if the wind freshens anywhere north to north-east. (4) In the south-east corner of harbour near breakwater.

It is best to enquire for a temporary use of mooring. There are a few white visitors' mooring buoys in the harbour, but if none is found vacant apply to the HM or the boatman at the yacht club. Yachts should be reported to the HM within 24 hours of arrival. In the event of gales from the north-west (which can occur suddenly if the wind veers at the end of a southerly gale) or north shelter should be sought at Torquay.

Facilities Brixham is particularly well provided with facilities for visiting yachts. There are banks, hotels, restaurants and shops of all kinds (EC Wed.). Upham's is a large yacht yard with four slipways and 10-ton hoist. Two other boat repairers. Two scrubbing grids 2m4 draught and eight scrubbing berths 3m0 draught by arrangement with HM. Also crane lift 4 tons at quay head. Compass swinging by arrangement with HM. Sailmakers. Water is obtainable by permission at the yacht club steps or at the New pier, where diesel oil is also obtainable. Petrol at garages, also water. In large quantities water and fuel may be obtained at the bunkering jetty. Customs Office. Yacht chandlers at quay and at Upham's. Launching sites: from south-east corner of outer harbour at all states of tide, breakwater hard slipway and from new slipway at Freshwater Quarry. Frequent buses to all parts and excursion boats to Torquay and Paignton. Yacht clubs: Brixham Y.C., Ibex S.C.

DARTMOUTH

Plan No. 34

High Water — *05 h. 15 m. Dover.*
Heights above Datum *MHWS 4m8. MLWS 0m4. MHWN 3m6. MLWN 1m8.*
Depths *Deep-water channel as far as Dittisham, but beyond this there are considerable variations in depth.*

DARTMOUTH is one of the most protected harbours on the South Coast. Shelter inside can be found in any weather, and if weatherbound, small yachts will find plenty of water to be explored within the harbour. Dartmouth is a town of character and the upper reaches of the Dart are beautiful. At HW navigation is possible as far as Totnes, some 10 miles up the river, in a vessel of up to 3m draught. Dartmouth is one of the West Country harbours offering the advantages that there is always room to bring up, and all the yacht clubs welcome visiting yachtsmen.

Approach and Entrance Dartmouth lies between the two promontories of Berry Head and the Start (see photographs under Passage Notes), being 5 miles from the former and 7 miles from the latter. The entrance is not conspicuous from seaward, but it can be located by the conspicuous 24m daymark (elevation about 170m) above Froward Point, east of the entrance, and the craggy Mewstone Rock (35m) and associated rocks.

The entrance is deep and well marked but there are dangers on each side. On the east side there are rocks to the west of the Mewstone; the Verticals (dry 1m8) and the West Rock with a depth over it of 0m9. South of Inner Froward Point is the Bear's Tail (dries 0m6) and 2¾ cables west of the Point is Old Castle Rock (with 1m8 over it), off which is the B Con Castle Ledge buoy. From about 3 hours flood to 3 hours ebb the stream sets towards these dangers, which should be given a

89. *Dartmouth Day Beacon situated north of Inner Froward Point. The Mewstone rises behind the small yacht. The photograph is taken with the day beacon bearing approximately north, distant 1 mile.*

wide berth. Approaching from the eastward keep the East Blackstone Rock (which is ½ mile east of Mewstone) well open of the Mewstone until the B Con Castle Ledge buoy comes in line with Blackstone Point on the west side of entrance.

On the west side of the approach there are rocks a cable off Combe Point and 3 cables off this Point is the Homestone (with 0m9 over it) marked by RW Cheq buoy. To north-north-east of this Point are the Meg Rocks which dry 3m0. Off Blackstone Point there is the Western Blackstone Rock, which can be seen as it is 2m high, but it has sunken off-liers.

Between the dangers mentioned the fairway is wide so that the approach is easy, except in strong south or south-east winds when a heavy swell runs into the harbour, reaching at times as far as the lower ferry. Meeting an *ebb* tide it can cause a dangerous sea for boats and small vessels. In the narrows there are two rocks to avoid on the west side opposite Kingswear Castle, the Checkstone (0m3 over it) and the Kitten rock (1m8 over it) south-south-east of the RW Cheq Checkstone buoy which lies off the ledges on the western side. The Kitten rock is on the edge of the fairway, so when approaching the narrows

keep well east of it and steer to give a good berth to the Checkstone buoy. The wind is often baffling and fluky in the narrows and their approach, but navigation is straightforward after passing the Checkstone and a vessel will proceed up the fairway.

Lights Enter in white sector of Kingswear light on east side of harbour. Iso W R G 3 sec. 26m 12M, W 325°–331°, R 325°–318°, G 331°–343°. The green sector covers dangers to port, and the red those to starboard. Alter course to port when white sector (289°–297°) of Dartmouth harbour light (Fl W R G 2 sec. 5m 6M) is entered and steer for it; thence steer up river between the shore lights of Dartmouth and Kingswear. When leaving Dartmouth steer on stern bearing in white sector of the harbour light. When the white sector of Kingswear light is entered steer out on it.

Anchorage and Moorings (1) Outside there is temporary anchorage in settled weather in the range but there is often an uncomfortable swell. It is prohibited in the area between Blackstone Point bearing 291° and Combe Point bearing 343° owing to cables which emerge seaward from

90. *The Mewstone and associated rocks from the southward.*

91. *Battery Point and Dartmouth Castle on west side of narrows, and the Checkstone buoy. (Photo : C. Sergel)*

92. *Dittisham, 3 miles up the River Dart on the west side.*

Compass Cove. (2) Anchorage available east of main channel opposite Dartmouth between line of large buoys and small craft moorings, but beware ground chain along line of large buoys. The Royal Dart Y.C. has six moorings, which if any vacant may be used by visitors on application to the Club. (3) Harbour Commission Moorings. These are marked D.H.C. and are available on the east side of the harbour and for smaller yachts on the Dartmouth side, on application to the HM. Berthing for short periods is allowed alongside the embankment wall, where there is also a scrubbing grid. Both embankments dry out at springs; the upper one beyond the pontoon (two F R at each end) also at Neaps. (4) Moorings and berths available at Dart Marina above floating bridge on west side, with petrol, diesel oil, water, yacht yard, hotel and facilities. Marina also has berths alongside floating pontoons up river off Noss Works. (5) Off Parsons Mud on the west side of the river between small craft moorings but note that cargo ships proceed all the way up the river and the channel must be kept clear at all times. (6) Greenway Quay, Dittisham. Some visitors' moorings off Ferry Boat Inn at Dittisham and off Stoke Gabriel; other moorings sometimes available by prior arrangement with HM. Anchor off Ferry Boat Inn below moorings. Fresh water tap on quay in front of the inn. LW landing pontoon at Dittisham for dinghies. Small passenger ferry operates between Dittisham and Greenway. Scrubbing alongside Greenway Quay by arrangement with ferry operator. Yacht yards in Galmpton Creek. Also anchorages off the upper boathouse between Sandridge Point and Galmpton Creek and upstream beyond Blackness Point.

Upper Reaches *See* Imray, Laurie, Moore & Wilson Y Chart No. 47. (a) If proceeding up river from Dittisham to the east of the Flat Owers Bank, keep all mooring buoys close to starboard to avoid the mudbank. (b) When there is sufficient depth of water to navigate to the west of the Flat Owers Bank, steer for the boathouse at Waddeton until the RW buoy is abeam to port, then alter course to port and steer for the upper Sandridge boathouse. When the upper Sandridge boathouse is abeam to starboard, alter course for Blackness Point, keeping Higher Gurrow Point fairly close to port. When Blackness Point is abeam to port, alter course for Pighole Point and leave all moorings close to starboard after passing Pighole Point. (c) If proceeding beyond Stoke Gabriel, when Mill Point is abeam alter course for the middle of the wood on the south bank of the river. Off the entrance to Bow Creek there is a BW buoy which is left close to starboard, then steer for the RW buoy off Duncannon. The river is marked with buoys and beacons to the end of Fleet Mill Reach after which the best water is approximately in the centre of the river to Totnes.

Make fast alongside in the Mill Tail which is the left hand channel on arrival at Totnes. The main river has two trots of moorings and a visitors' mooring is sometimes available by arrangement with the Totnes Boating Association. The Mill Tail dries out, the bottom being mud to a depth of about 0m5 and then sand. Attractive old town with castle. Boatyard. Chandlery. Hotels and restaurants. Shops.

Facilities Water point almost opposite Dartmouth Y.C. and by arrangement at Harbour Office at quays. At Dittisham public standpipes. Fuel at marina. Hotels and restaurants, good shopping centre—EC part Wed. part Sat. Customs House. Yacht yards, chandlers and all facilities. Yacht clubs: R. Dart Y.C. (Kingswear), Dartmouth Y.C., Dittisham S.C. Boatel with cabins and hire boats. Launching sites: public slipway at Kingswear next R. Dart Y.C., except near LW; slipway at Dartmouth dinghy basin, 2 hours each side HW or at any tide from slipway alongside upper ferry slipway, provided ferry is not obstructed. The nearest rail connection is at Paignton 7 miles (11 km) away. Buses to all parts.

SALCOMBE

Plan No. 35. Admiralty Chart No. 28

High Water   −05 h. 38 m. *Dover.*
Heights above Datum   *MHWS 5m3. MLWS 0m7. MHWN 4m1. MLWN 2m1.*
Depths   *On the leading marks the bar has a depth of 1m5, but the depth on the bar sometimes changes. Beyond the bar there is a deep channel as far as Tosnos Point in the 'Bag'. Above Tosnos Point are to Heath Point there is upwards of 2m with local knowledge, but strangers may not find more than 1m2 in parts. The estuary then shallows, but at three-quarters flood it is possible for vessels of 2m7 draught to navigate up to Kingsbridge, some 3 miles above Salcombe.*

Visiting yachtsmen consider that Salcombe is one of the best of the West Country ports. It certainly has a claim to this distinction for the harbour is lovely and is well sheltered. It offers anchorages and visitors' moorings, and is ideal for day sailing and boating of all kinds, and for family bathing, picnics and walks.

Approach and Entrance   The entrance is a simple matter with sufficient rise of tide on the bar and in the absence of strong onshore winds or swell.

The entrance is just to the east of Bolt Head, and some 3 miles west of the Prawle. Bolt head is a remarkable promontory with a spiked sky line. There are two islets, 'Mewstones', off the Point. A stranger might find some resemblance in profile between the Bolt and the Start, but the latter is a far longer headland and has a white lighthouse on it. (See Passage Notes.)

Strong southerly winds meeting the ebb at the Bolt set up overfalls which can be avoided by entering from farther east. The only dangers in the approach are rocks in the west side near the Mewstones which should be given a fair berth, and on the east side the Rickham Rock, which has 2m7 over it, and rocks near the coast farther eastwards.

Whether approaching from west or east it is simplest to alter course northwards about ¼ mile east of the Bolt. As the vessel sails northward, the small Starhole bay will be left to port where the remains of the wreck of the barque *Herzogin Cecilie* lie in the north-west corner under the high cliffs.

A headland on the north-east corner of this little bay with a detached rock (the Great Eelstone) will be observed. The Cadmus Rocks (0m3) lie south of Great Eelstone and must be avoided. The bar is situated about 2 cables north of the Great Eelstone Rock and the line of approach leaves the Great Eelstone about 1½ cables to port. The leading marks consist of a RW beacon with RW cage topmark on the Poundstone Rock (dries 4m) and a W beacon with a diamond topmark, situated in front of the left tangent of a big red-roofed house with two gables (see photograph). These bear 000° and if they cannot be located, a compass bearing on the left tangent of the house should suffice even if not affording the best water. There is also an approach across the bar farther to the east with a white house in line with the Poundstone beacon at 327°, but this is rarely used by strangers and carries less water.

The bar is dangerous in strong onshore winds especially with wind against an ebb tide, and has depths of 0m9 to 1m5 and less in some years. The bar should not be attempted under the conditions mentioned nor should it be crossed when a swell is running in until there is ample rise of tide over it. It is here that a lifeboat was lost. The entrance and bar are protected by land from the west and in normal conditions present no difficulties.

93. *The leading beacons almost in line with the left tangent of the red-roofed house with two gables.*

Once over the bar continue on the leading line leaving to port the Bass Rock (dries 0m9) off the next point, and to starboard the Wolf Rock (dries 0m6) marked by a B Con buoy. Course will then be altered to leave to port the Poundstone and two beacons off Sandhill Point and to starboard the light beacon marking the Blackstone Rocks. The reach to Salcombe is then plain sailing near mid-channel with the aid of the harbour plan.

Lights At Sandhill Point directional Lt Fl W R G 2 sec. 27m 10, 7, 7M. Approach in the white sector. When Blackstone beacon, (Qk Fl W R, R 218°–048°, W 048°–218°) changes from red to white the Wolf Rock has been cleared. Hold on course for ¾ cable until the leading lights up the river come into line at 042° but no farther. The front is Fl W 1½ sec. and the rear Fl W 3 sec. and they are situated on the east side of the Bag. They lead as far as the port hand ferry landing light F R and anchorage. It is possible to continue on the transit to the Bag by bringing the rear light just open to the right of the front one when passing Snapes Point; given sufficient moonlight to avoid the numerous yachts on moorings. On leaving Salcombe and proceeding down channel the cut of the W R sectors on the Blackstone beacon Qk Fl Lt provide an additional safeguard from shallow water on the south-east side. The cut in the sectors can also be used when entering once clear of all the Blackstone Rocks if the leading lights cannot be picked out among the riding lights.

Anchorage and Moorings (1) In the range outside the bar during offshore winds in settled weather, in depths as convenient. (2) Outside in Starhole Bay in 4 to 6m but avoid wreck extending a cable off north-west corner. (3) Large

94. *Salcombe as seen from the entrance of Southpool Lake.*

yachts usually bring up off the Marine Hotel, but it can be rough here in strong south-west winds. (4) Off the mud flats between Salcombe and Snapes Point. (5) Off Ditch End, on south side of the channel east of Salcombe. Convenient landing here, then short walk to ferry boat landing but visitors' moorings now occupy best positions. Take soundings to find position between deep channel and steep edge of the sands. (6) In the Bag, about ¾ mile north-west of Salcombe, but if anchoring take care to keep clear of moorings, with which the anchorage is crowded. (7) In the pool beyond shallow entrance of Frogmore Creek in 1m8. (8) *Moorings.* Salcombe is well provided with visitors' moorings with large white buoys numbered V1 to V22 which commence off the Marine Hotel and are situated each side of the fairway. All are capable of handling at least a 20-ton vessel and three between Scoble Point and Ditch End can accommodate 100-ton vessels. These can be used with permission of the Harbour Office or from harbour staff patrolling in launches marked 'Harbour Master', who can also find other moorings when vacant for visitors.

Creeks The arms and creeks provide a pretty and interesting cruising area for dinghies and shallow draught boats at HW, but the large-scale admiralty chart is desirable.

Southpool Lake, which joins the main channel opposite Salcombe, has uneven depths and the pools are occupied by moorings.

Frogmore Creek, which joins on the east side above Tosnos Point, also has an uneven bottom with depths ranging from a pool with 1m8 shallowing farther east to 0m3.

The upper reaches of the main channel are marked by posts on the mud on the port hand above Gerston Point and are navigable at HW to Kingsbridge.

Facilities   The principal facilities for visitors are centred near Whitestrand Landing Pontoon. HM's office (with VHF Radio). Water, diesel oil, petrol and chandlers nearby. Water also from water boat if bucket hung in rigging. Six yacht or boatyards. Grid. Launching slip 2 hours each side HW, and car park, though often crowded. Customs House opposite the Salcombe Hotel, and also in the town there are banks, hotels, restaurants and a good range of shops. EC Thurs. Hourly bus service to Kingsbridge. Yacht clubs: Salcombe Y.C. The Island Cruising Club invites visiting yachtsmen to use its club house at the north-east end of Salcombe. In rough weather, when dinghies are uncomfortable or unsafe, visitors may use the Club's launch service between Salcombe and the Bag by prior arrangement with the Club Office.

HOPE COVE

THIS cove lies just to the northward of Bolt Tail, and affords fair anchorage for yachts and small ships during winds from north-north-east to south-east in depths ranging from 10 to 4m. There are some ledges in the inner cove, and there is a drying harbour formed by a breakwater for boats. Three hotels. Village. EC Thurs.

YEALM RIVER

Plan Nos. 36a and 36b

High Water -05 h. 37 m. Dover.
Heights above Datum *Entrance MHWS 5m4. MLWS 0m7. MHWN 4m3. MLWN 2m1.*
Depths *0m6 on the leading lines on the bar but sands are always liable to change : thence not less than 2m1 to Yealm Pool.*

THE YEALM is one of the most beautiful harbours on the South Coast. The anchorage is sheltered and the entrance easy, except in strong onshore winds. It is not so well provided with facilities as Salcombe for example, but no cruise on the South Coast would be complete without putting into this secluded river.

Approach and Entrance The entrance is rough in strong onshore winds from the south-west, but under normal conditions with adequate rise of tide it is easy enough. The approach is made across Wembury Bay, which lies between Wembury Point on the north and Yealm Head on the south-east. From Wembury Head there are rocks and ledges extending $\frac{1}{2}$ mile south towards the conspicuous Mewstone Island, 59m1 high. On the south-west side of the Mewstone lies the Little Mewstone Rock (15m high) which has an offlying rock 50m off it awash at LW. Altogether the rocks or shoals extend 2 cables south-west of the Mewstone. In this vicinity there are tide rips when the wind is across the stream. A quarter of a mile eastward of the Mewstone lie the Inner (dry 3m0) and Outer Slimers.

Approaching from the northward or westward the Mewstone should be rounded at a distance of $\frac{1}{4}$ mile before altering course standing north-east into Wembury Bay to pick up the leading marks, taking care to leave the dangerous Outer Slimers (dry 1m5) to port.

When the entrance of the river is opened up, a house will be seen between trees near the summit on Misery Point (the inner point on the south side of the river) and below it, above Cellar Bay, a pair of leading beacons at 087° with white triangles with a vertical black line in centre. Bring these into line. After leaving Mouthstone Ledges to starboard keep slightly south of the transit, steering midway between their transit and the rocky shore on the starboard hand.

Approaching from the south or eastward give Gara Point a wide berth to clear the Eastern and Western Ebb rocks. Then come on to the leading mark which is Wembury Church (situated about a mile east of Wembury Point) bearing 002°. The Ebb rocks will be left close to starboard, but 005° gives better clearance. Hold on until the leading marks in Cellar Bay have been identified. Then alter course to their transit and proceed as before.

95. *The Mewstone from SW. This conspicuous islet lies on W side of Wembury Bay.*

96. *The first pair of leading marks are situated above Cellar Bay south of Misery Point in line at 087°.*

The bar lies south and south-east of Season Point with least water of 0m6 on the transit of the triangle-topped leading marks above Cellar Bay. When about 1½ cables off the lower leading mark course has to be altered to the next leading beacons which will be seen to the north-east on the hillside. These are white boards with line in centre and lead through the first bend in the channel at 048° but cross an inner arm of the bar with only 0m6, although slightly better water may be found close to starboard of their line. After that the river is clearly defined and it is merely necessary to keep near mid-channel taking care to leave to port the R W buoy on the north-side of the Pool. Note from the harbour plan that the deep channel is very narrow off the eastern extremity of Warren Point with only 0m3 on its west side and 0m4 on the east.

Above Warren Point, the Newton Ferrers creek opens out on the east side. It is wide but dries out at LW. The River Yealm itself continues above Warren Point first in a north-north-west direction and then bears through north to north-

97. *The second pair of leading marks are situated on the north slope to the right of clump of trees about 3 cables east of Season Point in line at 048°.*

east. The bottom is uneven, with depths of 3m4 to 1m8 for over ½ mile, but with shallower patches.

Anchorage and Moorings The Yealm has become so popular that moorings are laid in all the best parts and there is now no clear area left for anchoring in the Pool except in the fairway. Holding ground in parts of the river is poor and yachts should lay to two anchors, which should be buoyed if close to moorings. (1) Anchor outside in settled weather only, south-west of Misery Point off Cellar Bay in from 0m3 to 1m2 beyond the junction of leading lines, sheltered from east and south. (2) Anchor in the pool west of Warren Point. A number of moorings are available on application to the HM, including a trot south of Madge Point where yachts moor fore and aft and lay several abreast. (3) Note that anchorage is prohibited between the lower limit of oyster beds north of Madge Point and the upper limit east of Steer Point.

Facilities Water at private tap by Ferry Cottage near slip, or free at tap on ferry steps under Yealm Hotel. Stores,

98. *Ferry Point. Newton Ferrers. The Yealm Hotel and landing behind yacht in foreground. Continuation of Yealm River to left, Newton Ferrers creek to right.*

chandlery and PO at Newton Ferrers and Noss Mayo, also petrol and oil. EC Thurs. Scrubbing can be arranged. Two boat-builders. Hotels. Yealm Yacht Club. Newton Ferrers Sailing School who should be given consideration when practising. Launching sites: (1) Slip for launching at Bridgend Quay $2\frac{1}{2}$ hours either side of HW. (2) At the Brook, Newton Ferrers, same hours. (3) Also at Riverside road west $3\frac{1}{2}$ hours either side of HWS or $4\frac{1}{2}$ hours at HWN. HM at Newton Ferrers. Buses to Plymouth.

PLYMOUTH

Plan Nos. 37, 38, 39, 40. Admiralty Chart Nos. 1967, 1902.

High Water *Breakwater — 05 h. 49 m. Dover.*
Heights above Datum *Devonport: MHWS 5m5. MLWS 0m8. MHWN 4m4. MLWN 2m2.*
Depths *A deep water harbour used by large ships.*

PLYMOUTH is a naval and commercial port. The well-known anchorages are rather too exposed for small yachts in bad weather, but shelter can be found in the docks or up the rivers, with frequent bus services connecting with centre of the town. Cawsand at the west entrance and the Yealm River to the east are two of the pleasant anchorages conveniently near the town of Plymouth.

Inside the harbour is the River Tamar running northwards above Saltash, which is navigable and sheltered—the clearance under the high-tension wires 4 cables south of Cargreen is 30m, but looks less. The Tavy joins the Tamar about $1\frac{1}{4}$ miles above Saltash. This is a pretty river and though yachts cannot pass under the bridge it is navigable by small craft at HW, but note high-tension wires 12m clearance. Below Saltash the St German's (or Lynher) River joins the Hamoaze and extends in a westerly direction. The river is deep for about 2 miles and is navigable. Large-scale charts are required for navigation in these rivers. Plymouth harbour has developed greatly of recent years as a yacht and dinghy centre and there are more yacht and sailing clubs than in any other south-west centre.

The harbour is under the jurisdiction of the Queen's Harbour Master. There are bye-laws and prohibited anchorages situated principally in the main fairways. Yachts over 20m in length are subject to control by Traffic Signals displayed from the Longroom Port Control Station and Flagstaff Steps Signal Station during the movement of large vessels between the Sound and Hamoaze. Full details of the signals are contained in the *Channel Pilot* and the Dockyard Port of Plymouth Order 1975.

All small vessels are required to keep clear of large vessels which can only navigate in the deep water channels and civilian craft are required to give priority to warships at all times. The Longroom Port Control Station keeps a constant VHF watch on Channel 16.

Approach and Entrance Plymouth Sound lies between Penlee Point on the west and Wembury Point (off which lies the Mewstone) on the east. Within the Sound is a long low breakwater in the centre with channels each side of it. The principal approach to the harbour is through the western channel but the eastern channel is also navigable by day.

The Eddystone Rocks and Lighthouse are situated 10 miles off the entrance, and a course of 024° from the lighthouse leads to west breakwater head, which soon becomes conspicuous. From the westward a vessel will first pass Rame Head which appears as an almost conical promontory with the ruins of a chapel at its summit. A mile and a quarter east is Penlee Point, a low headland with a turreted beacon tower. The Draystone rocks (over most of which there is 1m8) extend $\frac{1}{4}$ mile to the south-east of Penlee Point, and are marked by a R can buoy. The western entrance lies only $1\frac{1}{2}$ miles ahead between Mount Edgecumbe and the breakwater. If the wind is light and off the land there are often pockets of calm or variable winds. After passing through the western entrance, Drake's Island will lie to the northward, distant $1\frac{1}{4}$ miles. The main fairway leads north-east and is marked on the port hand by the RW New Grounds and Melampus buoys towards the famous Plymouth Hoe (front) and thence through the Asia Pass. Yachts need not

99. *Plymouth breakwater at high water and West Head lighthouse. Staddon Heights in background.*

100. *Drake's Island from south and to right Plymouth Hoe.*

keep to the big ship fairway and can leave the buoys on the wrong side by reference to the chart. For principal buoys within the harbour see plan.

There is a short cut with 2m1 to the Hamoaze across the rocky ledge between Drake's Island and the Mount Edgecumbe shore known as 'The Bridge'. This channel is marked by a R can port hand buoy and B Con starboard hand buoy. As there are the remains of several dolphins in the vicinity of the entrance of the channel steer for it on a bearing of 332°, pass between the buoys and continue nothing west of the same course until past a RW buoy, after which the main Drake Channel is soon entered.

From the eastward the Mewstone (59m1 high) and the rocks south-west of it will be left to starboard. Next the Shagstone, off Renney Point (a nearly square rock 1m2 high marked by a black and orange beacon surmounted by a cone) should be given a good berth as the tide may be setting across the rocks between it and the shore. Continue northward passing between the breakwater (beacon at east extremity) and Staddon Point, leaving the coastline to starboard until the channel between Drake's Island and Mount Batten is approached. Here course may be altered to take the Asia Pass north-east of Drake's Island or the Smeaton Pass eastward of it or, if bound for the Barbican or Cattewater, hold on to Mount Batten breakwater end leaving it to starboard and the Mallard Shoal buoys to port. The passes are used by large ships, and as will be seen on the chart yachts need not adhere to them.

Lights At night enter by the western channel in the white sector of the West Breakwater Lt W R 10 sec. 19m 15–12M (W 262°–208° R 208°–262°). Bell 15 sec. The lower light in the window of the same structure Iso W 4 sec. 12M is useful if coming from the west of south-west as the sector (031°–039°) leads straight to the breakwater head leading past Draystone buoy (Gp Fl (2) W 5 sec.) south-east of Penlee Point. Keep a look-out for the Knap and unlit buoys. Within the harbour the edge of the cut of the white/red sector of W Breakwater Lt leads to the Melampus buoy (Fl R 4 sec.) after which refer to buoys (Fl R port and Fl W starboard as marked on the plan or preferably on the large-scale Admiralty chart). Within the harbour there are many directional lights, but these are intended for deep draught ships and, although their characters are shown, the sectors have been omitted on the small-scale plan already crowded with detail as their use is not necessary for the pilotage of smaller craft. At Mill-bay entrance the lights at west pierhead are two F R and at east pierhead F R and traffic signals; see below.

Anchorages and Moorings As Plymouth is a large harbour, the selection of an anchorage depends on wind direction and weather conditions. It is always wise to buoy the anchor. (1) Outside. Cawsand Bay is an excellent anchorage in winds from south-west to north-west. It has gradually shelving shores and offers good holding ground. (2) Off the north side of Drake's Island. Good holding, but exposed in unsettled weather. (3) Moorings on application off the Royal Western Yacht Club, or anchorage outside them in reasonable weather. (4) In the Cattewater (the easterly channel to the north of Mount Batten). Either off the Barbican on eastern side leading to Sutton Pool, or apply in Sutton Yacht Harbour for a pontoon berth, depths up to 1m9 MLWS. Moorings sometimes available on application to the yacht yard in Clovelly Bay, west of Turnchapel Point. If anchoring in the Cattewater buoy the anchor. (5) Anchor in Barn Pool, which is a bay sheltered from the west by Mount Edgecumbe. The bay is very deep, so work in well towards the shore and let go in about 4m5. Here also buoy the anchor as there is wreckage on bottom. Reverse eddy close inshore. (6) Off Cremyll, near the ferry, but the stream is strong. (7) Off Torpoint in the Hamoaze above the ferry-landing and sewer outfall, marked

101.   Royal Western Yacht Club of England (with flagstaff) and Plymouth Hoe.

102.   Entrance to Mill Bay dock is east of the conspicuous building.

by a noticeboard in 3mo. Avoid fouling moorings. (8) Mayflower Marina in Stonehouse Pool north-east of Cremyll. Deep-water berths for craft up to 21m length over all; forty-five visitors' berths. (9) Mill-bay dock. Subject to permission of the Dock Master (east side of entrance) and payment of dock dues, yachts may lock through near HW into the inner basin and lie alongside the quay. Entry signals: three black balls or three green lights vertical. Waiting trots in outer basin. There is complete shelter in the basin, all facilities and dock police in charge. Mill-bay dock is the best position for preparing to 'go foreign'. Provisions and bonded stores nearby, and Customs. Local shops and not far from centre of town. If leaving the yacht, arrangements for caretaking may be made.

Tamar River (for upper reaches see Y Chart No. 51)   Above Tor Point the river continues wide and deep and there are naval and reserve ships at moorings. Two miles up the river St German's River joins it on the west side, and $\frac{3}{4}$ mile beyond it is spanned by the high railway bridge and the road suspension bridge at Saltash. The entrance of the River Tavy lies $1\frac{1}{4}$ miles above the bridge, and here the River Tamar channel is narrow with depths as low as 1m8 near the starboard hand buoy, and wide expanses of shoal water on both sides. At Weir Point the river is spanned by high-tension cables with a clearance of 30m5. At a distance of $1\frac{1}{2}$ cables beyond the Point the best water 1m5 is only about 50 metres wide and a visiting yacht may cross a shoal in only 0m9, but the river deepens to about 4m5 off Cargreen. Above Cargreen the channel requires local knowledge as the best water is narrow between unmarked mud shoals. High-tension cables (19m2 clearance) span the river $1\frac{1}{4}$ miles beyond the village. The pretty upper reaches are navigable by shallow draught boats near HW. Principal anchorages: (1) Saltash on west side below or above the bridge in 6m or more. Anchorage prohibited in vicinity of water mains and cables. Facilities at Saltash. (2) Off Cargreen.

Water, facilities and inn.

St German's or Lynher River (see Y Chart No. 49)   The river is entered on the west side of the Tamar nearly $\frac{3}{4}$ mile south of Saltash bridges, leaving to port a RW buoy marking the flats and Beggars Island. It is buoyed as far as Forder Lake off which there is 1m8. Beyond this the bottom is uneven and nearly dries at LAT $\frac{1}{2}$ mile east of Earth Hill except for the Dandy Hole. Above Earth Hill the river is navigable in the dinghy or in shallow draught boats near HW. Principal anchorages: (1) Off the bay east of Jupiter Point but little room clear of Royal Naval moorings. (2) South-west of Forder Lake in 1mo to 3mo. (3) In Dandy Hole in 1m5 to 4m2 on south side of river south of Earth Hill and north of Warren Wood. This anchorage can only be reached at half flood, and soundings should be taken to find the edges of the pool. Two anchors necessary to restrict swinging and no facilities.

River Tavy   This shallow river is not available for yachts as it is spanned near the entrance by high-tension lines (12mo clearance) and by a railway bridge. There are extensive mud flats, but the river is pretty and navigable by dinghy or on the flood by shallow draught low-masted boats.

Facilities at Plymouth   Plymouth provides all facilities for anything from a dinghy to a man-of-war and the facilities of a large town. There are several yacht yards of which Mashford's at Cremyll is best known. Yacht clubs: R. Western Y.C. of England, R. Plymouth Corinthian Y.C., West Hoe S.C., Mayflower S.C., Laira S.C., Tamar River S.C., Saltash S.C., Torpoint Mosquito S.C., Cawsand Bay S.C. Launching site: the City Council has built a dinghy park alongside the Mayflower S.C., Barbican, which will accommodate about 300 dinghies. The Royal Western Y.C. and R.P.C.Y.C. have also a private slip for club members. Station and express railway services. Good bus services.

LOOE

Plan No. 41

High Water -05 h. 53 m. Dover.
Heights above Datum   *Outside MHWS 5m4. MLWS
0m6. MHWN 4m3. MLWN 2m0.*
Depths   *Harbour and entrance dry at LW. In anchorage
1m8 to 3m6.*

LOOE lies some 9 miles west of Rame Head and about 8 miles
east of Fowey. The harbour approach and entrance dry at LW;
Looe is not recommended in unsettled weather, as the
entrance becomes dangerous in strong onshore winds and
gales. The harbour itself is unsuitable for any yacht that cannot
take the ground, or lie against a quay. The anchorage outside is
a good one during offshore winds and is partially protected
from the south-west by Looe Island. Though crowded with
visitors in summer months, the town is pleasant, and the hiring
of boats and motor trips form a local summer industry.

Approach and Entrance   Looe is easy to locate because
Looe Island (St George's Island) is conspicuous off the
entrance. The principal danger in the approach from the
westward are the Rennies Rocks which extend south-east and
eastward of Looe Island. To clear them keep the beacon on
Gribbin Head open of the cliffs at Nealand Point (west of
Polperro) until the pierhead bears 305°, when steer for it.
There are tidal rips south of Looe Island and the Rennies
which in bad weather may be avoided by keeping farther
seaward. There is no passage suitable for strangers between
Looe Island and the mainland. Approaching from the
eastward, leave to starboard the red can bell buoy (unlit)

103.   Looe (St. George's) Island and Rennies rocks from east-south-east.

104. The harbour entrance dries out at LW.

marking Knight Errant Patch to the northward. Course may then be shaped from the buoy to the harbour entrance at 305°. On near approach to the harbour entrance keep clear of the Needles Eye, Chimney Rock and other rocks south of the entrance, and of the Pen Rock to the north. See chart for soundings. Just within the harbour entrance it dries 1m4. Wait for sufficient rise of tide. Off east quay there is a reverse eddy on the flood. There is a coastguard station on east side, from which storm signals are exhibited. Nearby a red flag is flown from a flagstaff when conditions in the bay are dangerous to shore boats.

Lights Lt Occ W R 3 sec. 8m 15, 12M at end of pier. Fog siren (2) 30 sec. sounded during fog when fishing and other vessels are at sea. Sectors: W 013° to 207°; R to 267°; W to 313°; R to 332°; obscured elsewhere. Approach at night in W sector 268° to 313° between the two R sectors.

Anchorage and Harbour Anchorage in the roadstead is good during settled weather in winds between west and north and in the absence of swell. There is wash from passenger launches and motor boats, as the roadstead is much used by pleasure boats. To avoid this and because the ebb runs fiercely out of the harbour and this torrent is felt for some distance

105. *Looe showing entrance, river and west quay. Yachts should anchor seaward of the launches in foreground. (Photo : Aerofilms Ltd.)*

seaward, anchorage to northward of the scour of the tide from the harbour entrance may be found better, say with the pierhead bearing about west by north, but keep well clear of the Pen Rock which lies a cable north-east. Depths range from 1m5 to 3 or 4m farther seaward. At Neaps it is possible to bring up much closer in.

Within the harbour there are long quays with 3m0 to 4m0 MHWS on the eastern side and 1m8 to 3m3 MHWS on the western. The harbour is often crowded by fishing vessels, and pleasure craft and boats, but the HM will direct to a berth.

Facilities Water at quays or fish market. Fuel and oil. Hotels and restaurants. Many shops. EC Thurs. Boat-builders and repairers and scrubbing. Launching site and car park on east side near flagstaff. Station and bus services. Yacht club: Looe S.C.

POLPERRO

Plan No. 42

High Water -05 *h.* 54 *m. Dover.*
Heights above Datum *approx. MHWS 5m4. MLWS 0m6. MHWN 4m3. MLWN 2m0.*
Depths *Harbour dries out but has 3m3 at MHWS and 1m5 at MHWN. Deepens to 2m5 in anchorage outside.*

POLPERRO is a small drying harbour 3 miles west of Looe and 5 miles east of Fowey. It lies at the end of an inlet between the cliffs extending about 3 cables in a north-westerly direction, and is protected by an outer pier and two inner piers between which is the entrance. This is only 9m8 wide and in bad weather was closed by baulks of timber but these are now replaced by a hydraulically-operated harbour gate. Polperro is a fishing village principally engaged in mackerel, pilchard and line fishing. There is no new chart of the harbour. The plan and soundings are based on a survey by Captains Williams and Bell, R.N. in 1857, coupled with observations by the HM. There appears to have been little alteration during the last 120 years, and the trawlermen confirm the soundings have not changed.

Approach and Entrance Approach should be made from a south-east direction when the harbour piers open up. As is shown on the plan, there are rocks extending to the Rannys (dry 0m8) off the headland on the west side of the entrance and there are also rocks at the foot of the cliffs on the east side. There is deep water up to the entrance of the inlet except for a rocky patch named the East Polca which lies a cable south-east of the entrance and has a depth of only 1m0,

106.   Polperro approach, anchorage and drying harbour. (Photo : Aerofilms Ltd.)

144

107. Polperro and harbour breakwater near LW.

but can be ignored in good weather with sufficient rise of tide over it. A rocky patch about 30m north-east of the Rannys can also be disregarded as this has a depth of 2m5 over it. When the promontory on the west side comes abeam the mid-channel depth is about 4m5 gradually shoaling to 2m5, 1m8 and 0m1 off the outer pier. The approach on a lee shore is dangerous in fresh south-east or southerly winds or when a swell is running in. Once within the entrance the inlet is protected from south-west through west to north-east.

Keep in mid-channel when within the inlet and approach the harbour entrance (with sufficient rise of tide) leaving the outer pier well to starboard and steering mid-way between the inner piers.

Lights and Signals   Spy-house Point east of the harbour entrance. Qk Fl W R 30m 8M ; W 060°–288°, R elsewhere. On west pierhead F W 4m 4M. When the harbour entrance is closed, a red light is substituted for white at the pierhead and by day a black ball is hoisted. Strangers should not attempt entrance at night.

Anchorage and Harbour   A few mooring buoys are laid just outside the harbour for mooring while waiting for the tide. There is also just room to anchor although the deep part of channel (2m5) is only about 25m wide. There are moorings inside the harbour but these are of use only to yachts equipped with legs, as the harbour dries out at least 0m6 MLWS. Yachts up to 12m in length are welcome in the harbour and at East Wharf there is a set of visitors fore and aft moorings 18m apart, which dry at LW on hard bottom against wooden posts. Steel ladders to quay.

Facilities   Water at fish market and on the quays. Fuel from Pearce Garage Ltd in village. Several small hotels. Shops. EC Sat. but usually open during summer months. Frequent buses to Looe and occasional to Polruan and Fowey. HM. Launching site on sloping beach at head of harbour.

FOWEY

Plan No. 43

High Water −05 h. 55 m. Dover.
Heights above Datum *MHWS 5m4. MLWS 0m6. MHWN 4m3. MLWN 2m0.*
Depths *At least 6m is maintained in the channel from sea to Wiseman Stone.*

FOWEY is an attractive west country port. It has a good harbour, available at all states of the tide and sheltered from gales except those between west-south-west and east-south-east. At such times there is a swell in the harbour, but shelter will be found farther up the river. The upper reaches offer pleasant dinghy excursions, though a look-out should be kept for squalls from steep slopes and sudden openings.

Approaches and Entrance Approaching from the eastward there is the dangerous Udder Rock (dries 0m6) situated 3 miles east of the entrance. This is marked by a R W Cheq bell buoy, and there are no dangers between this rock and the

108. River Fowey. Polruan Pool in foreground and Pont Pill Creek to right. Fowey town opposite on west bank of river. (Photo : Aerofilms Ltd.)

109. Polruan Point and Punch Cross white beacon on east side of entrance should be given a wide berth.

entrance except drying rocks off Pencarrow Hd. Fowey would not be very easy to identify from seaward but for the daymark on Gribbin Head, 1¼ miles south-west of the entrance, which must not be confused in thick weather with the old tower on Pencarrow Head, 2 miles east of Fowey. The Gribbin Beacon is a red and white tower 25m6 high standing at an elevation of 76m2 on a lofty headland, and is a conspicuous landmark when approaching from any direction.

From the westward avoid the Cannis Rock (dries 4m3), some 4 cables south-east of Gribbin Head. There are dangers south of the head so far as the Cannis Rock. There is a red can bell buoy off this rock, but to clear the danger keep the cross on Dodman Point open southward of Gwineas Rock.

Once past the Cannis alter course for the entrance, but as there are rocky ledges off the shore west of the entrance give this side a good berth until close to the entrance. Here the only dangers are the Punch Cross ledge on the east side, marked by a white cross (which should be given a berth of at least 6om) and the Lamp Rock marked with a white beacon nearly a cable beyond it and the Mundy Rocks opposite on the west side. Fowey is considered a good port to run for, but the entrance is of course very rough during onshore gales, and the seas break heavily in the approach with an ebb tide running against strong southerly winds.

Lights Approach in the W sector of Fowey lighthouse. Lt Fl W R 5 sec. 28m 11M until the W sector of Whitehouse Point

110. Polruan Pool is crowded with moorings. Buoy the anchor if room is found to anchor temporarily near them.

Lt (Iso W R G 3 sec. 11m 11, 8, 8M) within the harbour is picked up. Then enter in this sector. Once within the harbour the shore lights will be seen and there is a light F R on Whitehouse jetty, which should be given a good berth to avoid the unlit landing slip.

Anchorage and Moorings The river and harbour are under the control of the HM, who endeavours to meet the requirement of owners, though in the high season the most convenient berths are not always available. The harbour is used by large ships, and yachts must not anchor in any of the fairway, without prior consent of the HM, or in the swinging ground which lies off Pont Pill. Anchorages: (1) The Royal Fowey Y.C., which welcomes visiting yachtsmen, has five moorings on the Polruan side. If one is picked up temporarily the yacht must not be left unattended until application has been made and permission given by the Club, as the mooring may already have been let. Yachts should not anchor off the Club. (2) The area off Polruan is crowded with moorings but with the aid of the echo sounder it is sometimes possible to find a space for temporary anchorage out of the fairway and clear of vessels on moorings. It will be a poor anchorage because there are chains on the bottom so that anchors must have trip lines

III. Fowey Town. The Royal Fowey Yacht Club and landing is at the sea wall below the church.

and it can be rough on the ebb tide in strong south-west winds. (3) Just clear of the many moorings at Pont Pill, but it is essential to keep well clear of the swinging ground used by big ships. (4) In the pool above Wiseman Point in 3mo or more. This is a secure anchorage, though during gales there are fierce squalls blowing down from the hills. Unfortunately it is so crowded with moorings that it is usually difficult to find space to anchor. Enquiry can be made locally as to the possibility of hiring a mooring temporarily vacant. When proceeding up the river to Wiseman Pool keep a good look out for commercial traffic.

Upper Reaches   No difficulties are presented in sailing up the river as far as $\frac{1}{2}$ mile above Wiseman Point, but yachts under sail may find the wind heads and is fluky in some reaches. Near Bodmin Pill the channel becomes narrow and shallow and most of the river dries out at LW. It is navigable (with Y Chart No. 52) by shallow draught boats at HW as far as Lostwithiel, as also Penpoll and Lerryn creeks on the east side. These reaches are pretty and reward an excursion in the dinghy.

Facilities   Landing at Town quay. Water from R. Fowey Y.C. tap on the Town quay and a hose at Polruan quay; also large quantities may be obtained from E.C.C.'s Commercial jetties, first having made prior arrangements with their Berthing Master. Petrol and oil obtainable. Hotels and good shops. EC Wed. or Sat. Customs, HM and Lloyd's agent. Three yacht or boatyards. Scrubbing by arrangement at Mixtow Pill hard. Yacht clubs: Royal Fowey Y.C. and Fowey Gallants Club. Buses. Station at Par 4 miles (6.4 km) away. Launching facilities normally at Caffa Mill car park. Limited facilities at Polruan and at the Bodinnick Ferry Slipway, by arrangement with C. Toms & Sons. At Polruan there are small shops and hotels.

MEVAGISSEY

Plan No. 44

High Water −05 h. 55 m. Dover.
Heights above Datum MHWS 5m4. MLWS 0m7.
MHWN 4m3. MLWN 2m0.
Depths 2m1 at entrance, 1m5 to 0m9 in the centre of the harbour. The inner harbour dries out from 0m6 to 1m5 and more in some parts.

MEVAGISSEY is a pretty Cornish fishing village, with an outer and an inner drying harbour. The outer harbour is well sheltered by the land from prevailing winds from south-south-west to north-west. The northern pier protects it from the north except in very rough weather, but winds from any easterly direction bring in a swell. It is a bad harbour in strong onshore winds and gales, but Fowey provides a port of refuge only 7 miles distant, or Falmouth 14 miles.

Approach and Entrance The harbour is situated at the south side of Mevagissey Bay, a mile north of the low Chapel Point, 3½ miles north of the precipitous Dodman Point, and 2 miles south of Black Head. The Gwineas (8m high) and Yaw

112. Entrance to Mevagissey harbour. There are rocks north-east of the northern pier.

(dries om9) rocks lie south-west of Chapel Point, and are marked by a red can bell buoy Gp Fl (4), some 2 cables south-south-east of the Yaw. The entrance is easy in moderate weather, but it is only 50m wide, and there are rocks off the northern arm of the pier and a strong backwash when a swell is running. It should not be attempted in strong onshore winds.

Anchorage Anchor in outer harbour is 1m5, provided the wind is not onshore. In selecting position anchor clear of the moorings and do not obstruct the fairway, which is in constant use by fishing vessels. The best position is on north side of fairway, but anchor fore and aft to prevent swinging into the fairway. The HM will give directions. With easterly winds the swell enters and if strong the outer harbour is untenable for yachts.

Light Gp Fl (2) W 10 sec. 9m 12M from lighthouse at end of pier. Fog diaphone ev 30 sec. Occas.

Facilities Water at quay. Diesel oil, petrol, etc. at Marine Garage at inner harbour. Several small hotels and many shops. EC Mon. or Thurs. but some shops always open. Buses to St Austell, where there is a station. Boat-builder at Mevagissey, also yacht-builder at Portmellon, ½ mile southwards. Coast Guard and storm signals.

PORTMELLON

THIS little bay, ½ mile south of Mevagissey, provides a good, though rather narrow, temporary anchorage between the headlands. It is pretty and may be used during offshore winds in settled weather, taking soundings to find best position. There is a good yacht-builder (G. P. Mitchell) in the cove, and yachts are launched over the sea wall.

PORTSCATHO

A SMALL drying harbour on the west side of Gerrans Bay, situated about 3 miles north-east of St Anthony Head. It has a steep slip suitable for launching boats about 1½ hours each side of HW. During offshore winds and settled weather there is a temporary anchorage outside.

FALMOUTH

Plan Nos. 45, 46 and 47. Admiralty Chart No. 32

High Water   *+06 h. 12 m. Dover.*
Heights above Datum   *MHWS 5m3. MLWS 0m6.*
MHWN 4m2. MLWN 1m9.
Depths   *The eastern entrance channel is deep and the western over 5m ; Black Rock lies between the two and uncovers about half tide. The main channel River Fal has plenty of water for yachts as far as Maggoty Bank north of Ruan Creek.*

FALMOUTH, the historic Cornish port, is the most westerly of the deep-water natural harbours of the south coast. From time immemorial it has been used by sailing ships. The harbour and the neighbouring rivers and creeks provide one of the best centres for day sailing in the south of England. Falmouth itself is primarily a commercial port, equipped with big dry docks, but it is also an important yachting centre with first-class facilities of all kinds and in bad weather it is the most westerly large port of refuge on the south coast of England.

Just within the harbour entrance is St Mawes, which offers clean anchorages in beautiful surroundings. It has something of the attraction of Benodet on the Brittany coast. Between the Falmouth and St Mawes sides of the harbour is the northern arm, the River Fal which is pretty and provides interesting cruising and day sailing. It forks 5 miles up, the northern creek (Truro River) leading to Truro and the eastern one, Ruan Creek, forming a shallow continuation of the River Fal.

Approach and Entrance   The approach to Falmouth from the west or south is soon under the lee of the land in westerly and south-westerly winds after passing the Manacle

Rocks. It is also sheltered from the north, though steep seas may be found in the approach during strong winds.

The entrance lies within Falmouth Bay between Pendennis Point on the west and St Anthony Head on the east. It is a deep, easily navigated entrance but can be very rough during onshore gales blowing against an ebb tide.

Approaching from the eastward give the Dodman Point a berth of about 1½ miles, to clear the overfalls which, in bad weather, break over the ledges (The Field and The Bellows) some 6 to 7m deep. Also keep well away from Nare Head, for there are dangerous rocks (The Whelps, which dry 4m6) south-west of the Gull Rock. This rock is very conspicuous, being an islet 38m high, situated just over ½ mile east of Nare Head. Off the next point (Greeb Point) there are patches with only 3m7 to 4m6. Here also there are overfalls in bad weather over these the shoals known as 'The Bizzies'. Finally, if rounding St Anthony in very bad weather the overfalls over the rocky patches (with only 7m over them) can be avoided by keeping over a mile offshore, before altering course for the entrance.

In the entrance itself the only danger is Black Rock, which, as mentioned under 'Depths' uncovers at half tide. The rock is marked by a conspicuous black stone beacon, with globe topmark, and by a red buoy (Gp Fl W(4)) on its east-south-east. Black Rock lies a little westward of mid-channel and can be passed on either side, but the main channel is the eastern one.

After leaving Black Rock to port big ships also leave the West Narrows buoy Gp Fl (2) W 10 sec. to port and turn to the westward through the 5m8 dredged channel if proceeding to Falmouth docks, but most yachts can steer direct from off Black Rock in a least depth of 3m to join the dredged channel off the end of the Eastern Breakwater Docks Fl R 2 sec.

On the eastward side within the entrance lies the entrance to St Mawes Harbour. To enter this leave the black conical Castle

113.   On the right *is the eastern breakwater and docks. On the* left *is Falmouth inner harbour extending from the docks past the yacht club to Greenbank Quay facing Flushing. Beyond is the Penryn River. (Photo: Aerofilms Ltd.)*

114. Royal Cornwall Y.C. slipway on left, Greenbank on right. Yacht moorings extend from Prince of Wales Pier to yacht club.

buoy (Fl W 10 sec.) to port and steer between this and Carricknath Point (the point on the south of St Mawes River entrance). About 3 cables north-west of the Point lies an unlit RW Cheq buoy marking the Lugo Rock—which is dangerous, as there is only 0m6 over it. For buoyage within Falmouth Harbour refer to the plan.

Lights St Anthony Head. Lt Occ W R 15 sec. 22m, 22 20M. W from 295° to 004°, R to 022°, covering Manacles Rocks. W 022° to 172°. Fog Signal: Horn 30 sec. The Black Rock red buoy carries a Lt Gp Fl (4) W 15 sec. When entering at night give a good berth to St Anthony to clear the Shag Rock

and leave the Black Rock buoy to port, after which follow lights as shown on chart. A sharp look-out should be kept for unlit buoys, including the Governor and buoys off Falmouth.

Anchorage and Moorings (1) Outside: good holding ground, protected from west, suitable for large ships. (2) Carrick Road (centre of harbour) and above. This is used by large vessels, but there is a big swell in southerly gales. (3) St Mawes Creek. In offshore winds or settled weather there is a delightful anchorage about a cable south-east of St Mawes harbour in 1m2 to 2m4. Soundings should be taken as the depths shoal towards the shore and also in the direction of the

115. Mylor yacht moorings and harbour on the west side of River Fal.

116. Trelissick ferry landing on River Fal.

harbour. Tide is not strong inshore. Drying berths alongside quay in harbour but not much room. Water, fuel, hotels and shops. EC Thurs. Boat-builders. Ferries to Falmouth. Yacht club: St Mawes S.C. In bad weather with onshore winds proceed up river beyond Amsterdam Point. The area is crowded with moorings but the club has a mooring and if enquiry is made locally there is a possibility of finding a private mooring vacant. Likewise beyond Polvarth Point the Porthcuel river is full of moorings, so little anchorage is left clear of oyster beds. (4) Falmouth, off the town, temporary anchorage by permission of HM, but buoy the anchor, as the bottom is foul and there are moorings and chains. (5) Falmouth. The Royal Cornwall Y.C. has five moorings for visiting yachts. Apply to the Club for use of one if vacant. (6) Falmouth. Temporarily at Custom and North quays for provisioning, etc., where there is about 2m4, half flood to half ebb. Fresh water hydrant at North quay and shops at hand. (7) *Restronguet Creek* on moorings in deep hole west and south of Restronguet Point; avoid shallow patch at the entrance to creek. (8) Mylor Yacht Harbour consists of a small inner dock which dries, and an area north-east of it with over 220 swinging moorings, and depths ranging from 2m4 at the outer end down to 0m9 off the dock. There is about 1m5 LAT in the approach on the leading marks of three prominent trees centre of field to right of Mylor Creek with St Just village dead astern, but strangers best await more water. Facilities including chandlery near inner harbour. Yacht clubs: Mylor Y.C. and Mylor S.C. (9) St Just. Anchorage during north and east winds just inside point, also many moorings. (10) There are numerous anchorages in bays and bights in suitable wind conditions (some of which are mentioned below) but keep clear of oyster beds.

The Upper Reaches The upper reaches and creeks of Falmouth harbour offer interesting day sailing but a large-scale Admiralty Chart No. 32 is desirable as it is on five times larger scale than the harbour plan and shows every detail. At HW it is possible to navigate in the narrow buoyed channel as far as Truro where there is a quay, but at LW the river dries out below Malpas Point, south-east of which there are moorings and anchorage. On the western side of the main Fal

117. St. Mawes Harbour and to centre Polvarth Point and Porthcuel River. (Photo: Aerofilms Ltd.)

channel are Mylor Creek (already referred to) and Restronguet Creek (dries out except for deep hole inside entrance). Yacht club: Restronguet S.C. On the eastern side there is St Just Creek with 3m4 to 1m5 in anchorage and moorings area, but which dries out opposite the church. Ruan Creek, which is the eastern fork of the River Fal joining Truro River, is navigable for a short distance and there is anchorage near the entrance and small craft moorings farther east.

The Penryn River west of Falmouth carries over 2m and is buoyed for ½ mile above Greenbank Quay, as far as Boyers Cellars. At high water is navigable up to Penryn where there are quays and facilities.

Facilities at Falmouth Water from North quay, from Flushing quay or (by permission) from the yacht club. Petrol and oil, T.V.O. and diesel from pumps at North quay. Excellent shops including chart agents. EC Wed. or Thurs. Many hotels, of which the Greenbank is near the yacht club moorings and anchorage. Yacht builders and repairers, including Falmouth Boat Construction Ltd up the Penryn River north-west of Flushing, which has a fuel pontoon that is often moved down to Flushing at LW when the yard cannot be reached. Chandlery at yard and also at Falmouth Chandlers at Penryn. Customs. Railway station. Buses to all parts. Ferries to Flushing and St Mawes. Yacht clubs: R. Cornwall Y.C., Flushing S.C.

Launching Sites in Falmouth Harbour (1) At Falmouth, Grove Place Dinghy Park, in south-west corner of harbour. Launching hard accessible at all times except lowest spring tides for vessels up to about 9m long. Car park immediately adjacent. Changing and store rooms available at dinghy park. (2) At St Mawes, slipway at the harbour, which dries out. (3) Up the river at Porthcuel on east side of river, where road runs to slipway and beach. (4) At Mylor adjacent to the dockyard, car park, and at Mylor Bridge at end of creek, 1 hour each side of HW. (5) At Trenewth, south side of Restronguet Creek, road terminates at hard by sailing club. (6) Just west of the entrance of Pill Creek (¾ mile north-east of Restronguet Creek) slipway and car park.

Plan No. 48

High Water *Entrance +06 h. 10 m. Dover.*
Heights above Datum *Entrance MHWS 5m3. MLWS 0m6. MHWN 4m2. MLWN 1m9.*
Depths *Deep water in the approach; 3m1 on the bar, a mile inside the river. Beyond Navas Creek the river soon shallows and the bottom is uneven.*

HELFORD RIVER is very beautiful, and is one of the favourite yachting harbours of the West Country. The entrance is simple, the depth of water adequate for most small yachts and it is usually possible to get a mooring or find room to anchor. It is protected by land from all directions of wind other than easterly. Helford River and its various creeks offer a splendid expanse of water at HW for exploring in a dinghy and for picnics.

Approach and Entrance When coming from Falmouth keep on or east of a stern transit of the conspicuous Observatory tower at Falmouth in line with Pennance Point until Bosahan Point (on south side of river) is well open of Mawnan Shear (on north side of entrance). This will clear the dangerous Gedges Rocks, which lie between Mawnan Shear and Rosemullion Head on the north-east of entrance and are marked by a seasonal conical black buoy.

From the eastward keep in centre of entrance, but before approaching Bosahan Point give a good berth to the Voose rocks, marked by a beacon, some 4 cables eastward of Bosahan Point. Proceed through the 'narrows' and then avoid the shoal marked by a black buoy on the north side of the river opposite Helford Creek.

118.   Helford River facing west. Right *Mawnan Shear, Durgan Bay, Helford Passage, Porth Navas Creek*. On left *Bosahan Point, Helford Creek and Point*. *(Photo: Aerofilms Ltd.)*

119. Helford Creek and Village.

The leading marks up the river as far as Navas Creek were a white cottage in a group of buildings at Lower Calamansac which should be kept just open of the wooded point at Lower Calamansac. Entry is not difficult, even if these marks are not located, by keeping on the south side of the river off the ledges and leaving the black buoy, mentioned above, to starboard.

When coming from the west and south keep well clear of Nare Point and Dennis Head.

Lights None.

Anchorage and Moorings (1) Off Durgan anywhere clear of moorings in 1m3 to 3m4, exposed in easterly. (2) Off Helford. Excellent moorings of Helford River. S.C. or yacht yard on buoys marked for visitors, with moderate dues payable at shop at Helford Point. Or anchor if room in 3mo to 8mo. Strong stream. The mud south is very steep-to in places. Avoid cable crossing river near Bosahan Point, position marked by beacon on each side. (3) On moorings, if any available, across the bar in Pool just inside Navas Creek in 1m5 to 2m2. (4) On north side of river south of the bar and oyster buoys off entrance to Navas Creek. There are oyster beds in Navas Creek and off and west of its entrance and elsewhere, on which vessels must not anchor or ground. (5) In settled weather and offshore winds, in Gillan harbour (on south side of entrance) in 1m4 to 3m1 — poor holding ground and avoid the sunken rock in the middle of entrance.

Facilities Yacht club: Helford River S.C. At Helford there is a landing place at Helford Point (west of the creek), where water may be obtained from a tap at the shop which sells oilskins, clothes and other things. Boat-builders, and boats for hire. It is a short walk from Helford Point to the village, where there is a PO and shop; provisions and petrol may be obtained. Launching site at Helford village on south shore, where road crosses end of creek, at 1 hour each side of HW.

A ferry for pedestrians crosses the river from Helford Point to the Ferry Boat Inn at Helford Passage on the north side of the river, which is a hotel with restaurant. On this side of the river water may be obtained from a tap at cliff, 180m east of entrance to Navas Creek and also at Durgan. Buses to Falmouth from top of hill at Trebah, north of Durgan. Boat-builders and repairers at Helford and Porth Navas. Launching site at Helford Passage where road runs to water's edge by inn. Car park belongs to the inn. At Porth Navas there are dinghy landing, club, bar, shop, water, fuel and minor repairs.

COVERACK

Plan No. 49

High Water +06 h. 07 m. Dover.
Heights above Datum MHWS 5m3. MLWS 0m6.
MHWN 4m2. MLWN 1m9.

COVERACK COVE lies about 5 miles north-east of the Lizard, midway between Black Head and Lowland Point. The dangers in the approach from the south are The Guthens which lie off Chynhalls Point for a distance of nearly 2 cables and cover at high water. On the northward side of the cove there are ledges and rocks off Lowland Point, the most dangerous being the Dava rock, which extends 2 cables south of the Point, as it is awash at half tide. To the north-east lie the notorious Manacle rocks which are marked by a red buoy near their extremity. They should be given a good berth particularly if the tidal stream is setting towards them as they lie close to the direct line from Coverack to the buoy.

On the south side of the cove there is a small harbour, which is formed between the land and the pier, leaving an entrance 21m wide. The harbour dries out completely but at MHWS it has depths of about 3m5. It is very crowded with small craft during daytime but there is berthing accommodation at night for one yacht only up to 5 tons alongside the quay, preferably twin keeled. It is better to anchor outside given settled weather and offshore winds where it is sheltered from south-west to north-north-west.

Facilities Hotel and shops. EC Tues. Launching site on concrete ramp to firm sand.

120. *Coverack Harbour. There is one berth for a small yacht against the quay but a good anchorage to seaward in suitable weather.*

PORT MULLION (PORTH MELLIN)

Plan No. 50

High Water   *Lizard +05 h. 52 m. Dover.*
Heights above Datum   *Lizard MHWS 5m3. MLWS 0m6. MHWN 4m2. MLWN 1m9.*

THIS little harbour lies at the head of Mullion Cove, some 5 miles north-west of the Lizard. It is formed by two breakwaters, between which is the narrow entrance. The harbour dries out and could be used by berthing alongside the breakwater or quay, but only in exceptionally settled weather, with offshore winds. The cove and harbour are exposed to winds from all westerly directions, and, as even swell from the west causes a surge within the harbour, it would be an awkward place to be caught out in by a change in the weather.

121.   Mullion Island on right, harbour to the left off the dip in the hills. Note the conspicuous hotel on the left.

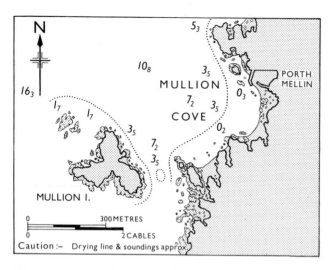

N

16_3

10_8

5_3

3_5

MULLION

0_3

PORTH
MELLIN

1_7

1_7

7_2

3_5

COVE

3_5

0_2

7_2

3_5

MULLION I.

| 0 | 300 METRES |
| 0 | 2 CABLES |

Caution :— Drying line & soundings approx.

122. Mullion harbour which dries out at LW.

Westerly swell again prevented the author from revisiting Mullion in 1975, but it is stated that the narrow entrance and harbour have been extensively rebuilt.

The anchorage in the cove is safer, provided it is used only in settled weather and offshore winds. It is open to the Atlantic from the west, and should be left immediately if the wind shifts or a shift is forecast to that direction. Anchorage can be found in the cove, taking soundings and bring up in 3 to 4m with the end of the harbour breakwater bearing approximately east Mag. The bottom is sand and rock. This anchorage is partly sheltered from the south-west by Mullion Island, but not sufficiently to make it a safe anchorage in winds from this direction.

There is a café at Port Mullion where some stores may be obtained. Road leads to steep beach where launching possible at HW. Car park. There are shops, a garage and 'pub' at Mullion village, situated at the end of a rather uninspiring uphill walk of a mile from the pretty little cove. EC Wed. Launching site on hard beach exposed below ramp.

PORTHLEVEN

Plan No. 51

High Water *+05 h. 51 m. Dover.*
Heights above Datum *MHWS 5m5. MLWS 0m8.*
MHWN 4m3. MLWN 2m0.
Depths *There is 1m2 in the approach and 2m3 in centre of the entrance north-west of pier, but dries out above the lifeboat house.*

THIS small tidal harbour is situated 8½ miles north-west of the Lizard and may be located by a clock tower, a flagstaff and the white houses in the background which are conspicuous from a considerable distance. The approach and entrance are open to the west, south and south-east. The port used to be entered by coasters but this trade has almost ceased and it is used principally by small fishing vessels. Porthleven is rarely visited by yachts. It provides only drying berths alongside the quay in the inner harbour.

Approach and Entrance The entrance lies between the rocks off the pierhead on the south-east side and the Deazle Rocks on the north-west side. It is considered a difficult entrance because it is only 60m wide and the Deazle Rocks are not marked by buoys or beacons, nor are there clear leading marks to lead up the centre of the entrance. Pilotage used to be compulsory and it would be undesirable for a stranger to attempt the entrance without local advice except under

123. *Porthleven outer harbour near high water. Rocks dry at LW 50 metres or more SW, South and SE of the pier head.*

124.   *Porthleven harbour near LW. Note the rocks off the pier and fringing its inner side. Fishing vessels lie near centre of outer harbour. With sufficient rise of tide pass between the short inner piers bearing to port to the inner harbour if HM has a berth available. (Photo: Aerofilms Ltd.)*

particularly favourable conditions in offshore winds and in the absence of swell. The following information is based on the author's experience when visiting the harbour by sea, but has not been checked by the HM.

Approach should be made on a course parallel with the long inner side (not the short arm at the end) of the pier, but about 20m north-west of it on the line of soundings 3m5 to 1m5 on the plan. This course crosses a bar formation (which is liable to change) in about 1m2 LAT. At the entrance there are ledges of rock extending about 50m or more off the pier and from south-west to south-east. The entrance thus lies between these rocks on the east side and the Deazle Rocks on the west. There is 2m3 at the entrance but it soon shallows within. Fishing boats will be seen on moorings in the centre of the outer harbour but most of these nearly dry out at MLWS. Fishing boats proceed in or out of the harbour fairly frequently, and if in doubt advice may usually be obtained from one of them. When the harbour is closed this is indicated by the hoisting of a red ball on the flagpole at the inner end of the pier; at night when the harbour is closed the two red lights are not shown.

Lights   There is an Occas F R Lt 10m 4M which is situated about 30m from the pierhead. A second Occas Lt F R has been placed on the east side of the harbour vis. 057°–075°. Approach at night would be dangerous for strangers.

Harbour   Except in the pool near the entrance the outer harbour dries 0m9 to 1m8, and there are rocks fringing the foot of the pier. The inner harbour lies beyond the inner pierheads, and the entrance can be closed with baulks of timber in bad weather. The inner harbour dries out completely, but by arrangement with the HM there are berths alongside the quay where yachts can lie with about 3m at MHWS in the deepest berth.

Facilities   Water, fuel and some stores. EC Wed. Boat-builders. Two small hotels. Good bus service to Penzance and Falmouth and district. Launching sites: trailed boats of any size from ramp, slipway at the head of the inner harbour for launching small craft by hand near HW.

Plan No. 52. Admiralty Chart No. 2345

High Water   +05 h. 50 m. Dover.
Heights above Datum   *MHWS 5m6. MLWS 0m8. MHWN 4m4. MLWN 2m0.*
Depths   *The harbour dries out but there is about 3m3 at MHWS.*

St michael's mount, with the castle at its summit, is one of the strangest and most romantic looking formations off the south coast of England. From A.D.25, when it was used by Mediterranean merchants as a base for tin trading, its long and varied history is of great interest. It is now National Trust property and it is well worth making a point of sailing there if the weather is suitable.

The Mount is conspicuous from seaward. There is a small drying harbour at the north end which is formed between two piers and there is anchorage to the westward of the entrance.

Approach and Entrance   Approach may be made with the aid of the large-scale Admiralty chart from the direction of the Gear Rock beacon off Penzance steering on the line to the north end of the harbour breakwater at 074°. The principal dangers in the approach are the Hogus Rocks which form a large expanse of reef to the north-west of the harbour, and the Outer Penzeath Rock, with less than 2m over it, which lies about 3 cables west-south-west of the Hogus Rocks. These dangers are left to port. Nearly a cable south-south-west of the Mount lies the Maltman Rock which dries 0m9, but this needs to be considered only if approaching from south or south-east. The various rocks have no beacons to mark them and some

125. St. Michael's Mount from the SW.

126. The harbour at St. Michael's Mount.

yachtsmen consider that the harbour should not be attempted by a stranger without the aid of a pilot. However, in reasonable weather with a leading wind and an accurate compass the approach can be made given due caution.

The approach gradually shelves from 8m to 2m a cable west of the entrance. Depths then rapidly fall and the bottom dries

out northward of the west pier. Do not leave the pier more than ½ cable to starboard as the Hogus Rocks lie only a cable north of it. Then enter with sufficient rise of tide.

Alternatively, approach may be made from the south. Keep well away from the rocks extending south of the Mount. Then follow up the west side at a distance of about one cable, but note a rock (2m1 over it) and an obstruction (2m4 over it), dangerous in a bad sea or swell. When the pierhead bears 060° steer into the anchorage or, with sufficient rise, steer direct for the pierhead and enter.

Lights   Approaching from Penzance the division of the red and white sectors of Penzance south pier light leads south of the dangers to the northward and a little south of the entrance to St Michael's harbour. There are no lights at the harbour so strangers should not attempt the passage at night.

Harbour and Anchorage   There is a pleasant anchorage in 2m7 about a cable west Mag of the northern end of the west pier, which can be used in settled weather sheltered from north through east to south-east. The entrance between the piers is 30m wide and the harbour dries from 1m5 to 3m0. There is a HM who will direct a visiting yacht to a drying berth, usually alongside a ladder on the west quay as the east quay is in active use by the ferries and launches.

Facilities   There are no facilities on the island except water and a café (open Mondays to Fridays in summer months), which supplies a few simple provisions, but all facilities are available at Marazion, ½ mile to the northward. This can be reached across the causeway at LW or by dinghy or ferry at HW. Water, fuel, hotels, banks, shops. EC Wed. but some shops open on all days. Yacht club: Mount's Bay S.C. Facilities for dinghy racing. Launching site: at the west end of Marazion on beach, with car park and garage adjacent. Frequent bus services.

PENZANCE

Plan No. 53

High Water +05 h. 50 m. Dover.
Heights above Datum *MHWS 5m6. MLWS om8.
MHWN 4m4. MLWN 2mo.*
Depths *There is about 1m8 in the approach to the south pier.
The outer harbour dries out completely, except in the narrow
channel along the south pier where the depth outside the locks is
om6. There is usually not less than 4m2 of water in the inner basin,
which is open for about 2 hours before HW to HW.*

PENZANCE is a commercial harbour but it is also frequently
used by yachts. It is a useful port of departure for Ireland, the
Irish Sea and the Scillies. In strong winds and gales from the
south and especially from south-east it is dangerous to run for
shelter at Penzance owing to the shoaling water in the
approach and because the lock gates cannot always be opened.
Mount's Bay is very exposed to winds from these quarters.

Approach and Entrance Penzance lies in the north-west
corner of Mount's Bay some 15½ miles north-west of Lizard
Point. A yacht coming from the eastward should keep 2 to 3
miles off the Lizard in rough weather (see Passage Notes) or in a
fresh wind contrary to the tide to avoid the overfalls and should
shape a course outside the Boa shoal (3 miles west of the
Lizard). On nearer approach to Penzance Bay there are shoals
to the southward of Cudden Point which may be avoided by
keeping west of the transit of the tower on St Michael's Mount
and Ludgvan church at 340°.

Coming from the westward after passing the Runnel Stone
follow up the coast keeping a mile offshore as far as St
Clement's Island. Leaving the island about 2 cables to port
make good 020° leaving Low Lee RW Cheq buoy to port,
where bring Penzance South pierhead bearing 350° and steer
for it. Give a good berth to Gear Rock ½ mile south of the pier
(which is marked by a black beacon with cage topmark) and to
the Battery Rocks to south-west of the pier. Then round in
towards the pierheads. Note that at LW springs there is only
about 1m8 east of the south pier and see 'Depths' for water
within harbour. Half a mile north-east of the entrance lie the
Cressar Rocks marked by a BW beacon.

Lights Penzance South Pier lighthouse has a Lt Gp Occ
(2) W R 15 sec. 11m 9, 8M. Fog Reed (2) 30 sec. Approach in
the W sector. The R sectors on each side cover the outlying
dangers, but the western edge of the white sector cuts close to
Gear Rock.

Tidal Signals from flagstaff on south pierhead. 4m5
water or over at pierhead: day, a ball; night, red light. Dock
gates open: day, two balls, horizontal; night, two red lights
vertical. Dock gates closed or not to open: day, two balls
vertical; night, red light over green light. When the dock gates
are open a green light is shown from north dockhead, and a red
from south dockhead.

Anchorage The large outer harbour on the north side
dries out at W. Here there are many moorings for dinghies and
small craft which can take the bottom at LW. It is not suitable
for keel yachts although it is possible to dry out alongside the
south quay or alongside the Albert pier, subject to the prior
rights of the *Scillonian*, which is the safer location outside the
basin. It is far better to enter the inner basin, where there is
usually about 4m2 of water. As mentioned above, the dock
gates open from 2 hours before HW to HW. In strong
southerly gales the seas break over the south pier of the basin,
so the north pier is the better for shelter, although here there is
often coal dust.

127. Penzance from SE. The approach, locks at entrance to inner basin. In background, Albert Pier and outer harbour which dries out. (Photo: Aerofilms Ltd.)

Waiting for tide, anchor outside about 2 cables south-east of the south pierhead, weather permitting.

Facilities Water at quay. Customs. Two boatyards; scrubbing at hard in outer harbour. Fuel, chandlery and sailmaker in the town. Many hotels, restaurants, shops of all kinds. EC Wed. Yacht club: Penzance S.C. Launching site: dinghies may use the slipway at the outer harbour approximately from $3\frac{1}{2}$ hours before to $3\frac{1}{2}$ hours after HW. Station and buses to all districts. Passenger ferry and helicopter service to Scilly Isles.

NEWLYN

High Water +*05 h. 50 m. Dover.*
Heights above Datum *MHWS 5m6. MLWS 0m8.
MHWN 4m4. MLWN 2m0.*
Depths *The entrance has been dredged to 3m9 and for about
130m vessels drawing 3m3 can lie alongside the north pier. The
harbour shallows progressively farther northwards, with 1m8 at
the third tier and drying at the end.*

NEWLYN is a sheltered harbour but southerly and south-east
winds can bring a heavy swell outside, and the approach would
be very dangerous in a south-east gale as it would then be on a
lee shore. It is inconvenient for yachts not equipped with legs,
as it is a busy fishing port with limited room to lie afloat
alongside the north-east quay. The HM always endeavours to
find a place for a visiting yacht, but this is not always possible
free from disturbance by other vessels during the pilchard
season in June, July and August. Then the harbour has to
accommodate fishing vessels from Looe, Mevagissey and St
Ives in addition to its own fleet. The south pier has 3m9 at its
extremity, but should not be used by yachts as it is reserved for
stone ships and commercial vessels.

The best way of visiting Newlyn in offshore winds is to
anchor outside in Gwavas Lake and enter the harbour by
dinghy.

Approach and Entrance Coming from west or south
follow the instructions given for Penzance, but alter course for
Newlyn when the pierheads bear 270°, distant about ¾ mile. If
coming from the east follow the instructions for Penzance but

128. *The spar buoy within the entrance which is left to port.*

129. *Course is altered to starboard. The channel lies between fish quay
to starboard and edge of dredged channel to port, in line with two posts
with boards on fish market.*

alter course when Newlyn bears 270°. Enter between the
pierheads, when a small RW spar buoy will be seen ahead.
This marks the end of a slipway, and course should be altered
to starboard to leave the buoy to port. The west side of the
harbour dries out, but there is a dredged channel for about a
cable on the east side parallel with the north pier. The west side
of this dredged channel is marked by the transit of two rather

inconspicuous R W leading boards on posts situated on the fish market.

Lights South pier lighthouse: Lt Fl 5 sec. 10m 9M, 253° to 336°. Fog siren 60 sec. North pier: F R 2M, 238° to 248°, W over harbour. Slipway spar buoy has R W Scotchlite reflectors. Two R Lts are sited on the leading boards marking the west edge of the dredged channel. Also a small R Lt on old quay.

Anchorage and Harbour (1) Outside in Gwavas Lake in offshore winds; east of the south end of the north quay, clear of the fairway in 2m1 or more farther seaward. Good holding ground and well sheltered from south-west, through west to north-west. (2) Lay inside alongside outer half of north pier or abreast of other vessels but apply to HM for berth, least inconvenienced by movements of fishing vessels. The best water is 3m3 at the outer end but the berths are in frequent use by the big fishing vessels. A cable from the entrance the depth is 0m9 LAT plus 0m8 at MLWS, +2m0 at MLWN. Legs necessary when not alongside as no room elsewhere to lie afloat. Owing to the increasingly large number of fishing vessels based at the port, masters or owners of visiting yachts are asked to keep sufficient crew on board to move the vessel if requested by fishing boats. When the local fishing fleet is forced to return through stress of weather all berths at Newlyn are required by them and yachts are asked to seek shelter at Penzance.

Facilities Water by hydrants at all berths. Diesel oil hydrants and petrol at Ridges on the quay. Custom House. Two ship and yacht repairers, J. Peak & Son and H. N. Peak. Slipway up to 27m4 keel, 6m4 draught available at reasonable rates on application to HM.

Three small hotels. Shops. EC Wed. Frequent buses to Penzance and elsewhere. Station at Penzance. Launching sites: by arrangement with HM only, as the harbour is in continuous active use by fishing vessels.

MOUSEHOLE HARBOUR

Plan No. 55

High Water *+05 h. 50 m. Dover.*
Heights above Datum *MHWS 5m6. MLWS 0m8. MHWN 4m3. MLWN 2m0.*
Depths *Dries out at LW. At MHWS there is about 4m8 and MHWN about 3m5. Bottom gravel on rock.*

MOUSEHOLE HARBOUR is a small drying harbour formed by two breakwaters leaving an entrance only 11m wide. The harbour is well protected except in strong winds between south and east. The harbour entrance can be closed with baulks of timber. The harbour and village are picturesque and much frequented by artists. There is an anchorage outside during offshore winds.

Approach and Entrance Mousehole is situated 1¼ miles south of Newlyn and lies west of the small St Clement's Island, which makes it easy to locate. St Clement's Island is fringed with rocks as shown on the plan, and the easiest approach to the harbour is from the southward, following parallel with the line of the Cornish coast to port, and passing rather west of midway between the shore and St Clement's Island. Once the middle of the island is abeam the water between the island and the harbour is clear of dangers, apart from the rocks fringing the seaward sides of the breakwaters. Depths in the approach vary from 6m7 when St Clement's Island is abeam down to about 0m5 off the entrance, where with sufficient rise of tide final approach should be made when the centre bears 270°, distant ½ cable.

Lights Two W Lts are exhibited on the northern pier

130. Mousehole harbour at low water. (Photo : Aerofilms Ltd.)

head, but when the harbour is closed a R Lt is substituted.

Harbour and Anchorage Yachts dry out alongside the inner sides of the breakwaters and the deepest berths are near the entrance. There is a HM who will give instructions for berthing and his assistance should be sought as nowadays the harbour is so crowded with small craft that it is difficult to get alongside. The anchorage outside provides good holding ground. It is sheltered by the land from north and west and St Clement's Island provides partial protection from light east winds, but it is open to south and south-east which are dangerous quarters in unsettled weather. Even with westerly winds there is sometimes swell entering the anchorage from the south. Take soundings to find best position to anchor, approximately midway between the south breakwater and the middle of the island.

Facilities Water and petrol. Three small hotels, several shops. EC Wed. Launching site: slipway in harbour. Car park nearby. Buses to Newlyn and Penzance.

ISLES OF SCILLY

Plan Nos. 56, 57 and 58. Admiralty Chart No. 34

High Water *(St Mary's Pool) +05 h. 52 m. Dover.*
Heights above Datum *MHWS 5m7. MLWS 0m7. MHWN 4m3. MLWN 2m0.*
Depths *Up to 2m1 in St Mary's Pool. 2m4 to 11m0 in anchorage north-west of New Grimsby harbour (Tresco).*

THESE islands—some forty-seven of them—have a charm that only a personal visit can reveal, they are a 'cocktail' with ingredients from England, Scotland, Brittany and the tropics.

Only five islands, each so different from the others, are inhabited—St Mary's, Tresco, St Martin's, Bryher and St Agnes; of these St Mary's is the biggest with Hugh Town built around the harbour as its 'capital'.

Any yacht exploring these islands should have the largest scale Admiralty charts aboard. The charm of this archipelago should not lull the navigator into a false sense of security as there are many hidden dangers in the form of pinnacle rocks with strong tidal eddies around them. Local knowledge is very desirable if any intricate passages between the smaller islands are contemplated. Here only the safest four, of the six, approach channels to St Mary's Road will be described.

Off-lying Dangers These are numerous and clearly marked in the Admiralty chart. All rise suddenly from deep water; mentioned here—only because of their isolation in the extreme west—are the Crim Rocks (2m0) and others near them lying about 1½ miles north of the Bishop Rock. Approach into these islands in thick weather is extremely dangerous and the greatest caution is needed if the distant leading marks cannot

be seen. If in doubt lay-off. The approach to St Mary's Road from the east, which is recommended locally, is by way of St Mary's Sound which is clearly marked. Alternatively approach can be made in suitable weather to Crow Sound from the south-east provided the wind is offshore, the bar is not crossed and one anchors to the east of the Hats buoy. At night also, if seeking a lee on the east side of the islands it may assist to note that Peninnis light becomes obscured on a bearing of about 231°. However, the navigation at night is not recommended in the absence of local knowledge.

Approach Channels from the East

Crow Sound (view A) The flood tide flows into here, thus the Hats buoy (B Con with triangle topmark) is left to

131. Round Island. This island, situated on north side of the Scillies, is conspicuous by its shape and white lighthouse at its summit. (Photo: Aerofilms Ltd.)

132. *A. Crow Sound. Innisidgen in front of distant Crow Point, Tresco.*

133. *B. St. Mary's Sound. Gt. Minalto on front of Mincarlo.*

134. *C. Broad Sound. Bant's Carn (St. Mary's) in front of Gt. Ganilly Telegraph Tower. St. Mary's is on right and Crow Rk beacon with distant St. Martin's is on left. Detached distant island in Nornour.*

135. *D. North Channel. Gt. Smith rocks in front of old lighthouse on St. Agnes.*

136. *E2. One of the two clearing marks for Woodcock Ledge—the Creeb Rocks in line with right extreme of St. Martin's.*

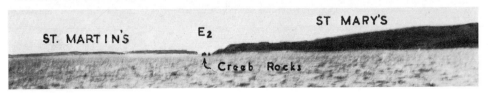

137. Hugh Town harbour, St. Mary's. The anchorage (often crowded) lies E and NE of a line from well off the pier head to just east of the lifeboat slip. (Photo : Aerofilms Ltd.)

starboard, after which the transit is left and the rock (dries om6) off Innisidgen Island (7m0 high) given a clear berth if near LW. The Crow Bar sands, formerly om9, have moved and increased. Entry should not be attempted at Springs until there is ample rise of tide and the best water will be found at the point where sand and weed join, which can usually be seen in the clear water.

St Mary's Sound (view B) Approach from the south-east to avoid Gilstone (dries 3m9). The transit marks may be a little difficult to pick out but there is deep water close to the south of the rocky Peninnis Head with lighthouse (Fl W 15 sec. 36m 20M) set back and a red bell buoy marks the Spanish Ledges to port. However, care should be taken when to the south of Garrison Hill not to get too close to the Woolpack beacon as there is a om7 patch ½ cable west of it. After leaving the Bartholomew R buoy to port, round slowly to the north-north-east; deep draught yachts may want to take note of the clearing marks (E1 and E2 on the plan) for the Woodcock Ledge with 2m7 over it.

Approach Channels from the West

Broad Sound (view C) The leading transits are rather far distant and may not be visible. However, the channel is buoyed starting with Flemming's Ledge (R buoy) to the north of the Bishop Rock lighthouse, after which the Gunners buoy (RW Cheq) is left to port. Next make for the Old Wreck B buoy, leaving it to starboard, but take care to keep clear of the Jeffrey Rock (om9) if of deep draught. The leading marks should now be visible and they will take the vessel clear to the south of Spencers Ledge (2m7) and the Southward Well (dries 1m5) respectively 8½ cables to the south-west and 4 cables to the south of Sampson.

North Channel (view D) A cross tide may be experienced in this channel, but given reasonable visibility the leading marks are good. The main danger is Steeple Rock (om4) which

is over 6 cables south-west of Mincarlo and is left less than 2 cables on the port hand when on the transit. Keep on the transit until the Broad Sound transit is picked up.

Entrance to St Mary's Pool and Harbour Once in St Mary's Road, most yachts will wish to bring up in the pool or harbour. The only danger is the Bacon Ledge (om3), or Pool Ledge; the former is flanked on the north-east by The Cow, which dries. Of the two leading marks illustrated, the southernmost one—view F—is perhaps the more easily distinguished.

The limits of the anchorage for visiting craft are roughly a line (shown on plan) from off the quay head to just east of the lifeboat slip. Yachts should anchor to east and north-east of this line clear of the line of the lifeboat slip and well clear of the northern end of the area, leaving plenty of room for the *Scillonian* to turn.

An Alternative Anchorage If a blow from the south-west is likely, larger yachts which may have brought up in St Mary's Road would be wise to leave by St Mary's Channel and anchor in Crow Sound off Watermill Bay to the north-east of the island.

Facilities Although the smaller inhabited islands have very small village stores, Hugh Town on St Mary's offers much in the way of mainland facilities such as a PO, chemist, hospital, provision stores, banks and a few hotels. Water, petrol, gas and diesel oil at quay. Boat repairing by Mr S. G. Ellis, Mr T. H. Chudley or the Isle of Scilly S.S. Co. Engineers H. Taylor, Hugh Town and D. Parr, Porth Mellon. Outboards and chandlery, etc. South'ard Sailing. Customs. A bus runs to the airport from which there is a fairly frequent daily helicopter service to Penzance (booking always required). Daily steamer service runs each afternoon in the summer to Penzance. Yacht club: Scillonian Sailing and Boating Club.

138. F. *Entrance to Hugh Town harbour—Old Man beacons in line: front now white pole and triangle top, rear W pole and St. Andrew's Cross. (Note lifeboat slip on right.)*

139. G. *Alternative entrance to Hugh Town harbour—Buzzer Mill in line with Old Smithy (white gable end).*

140. *New Grimsby Sound. H. Leading line—Hangman's I. west side in line with Star Castle on distant St. Mary's.*

New Grimsby Harbour—Tresco See Admiralty Chart. This island is justly famous for its tropical gardens and many yachts like to bring up in the passage between the island and Bryher. The entrance from the north-west is a little tricky and should only be attempted for the first time in favourable weather conditions with a leading wind or under engine. Clear of the north-west entrance a flood tide, north-east going, of 2 to 4 knots may be experienced. Keep on the transit (see view H) and give particular attention to the Kettle and Kettle Bottom Ledges which dry little over a cable to the north-east at the entrance, and also to a drying rock which is inside the entrance but scarcely ½ cable to the north-east. There is a deep anchorage in 11m between Cromwell's Castle and Hangman Isle; after this the bottom shoals to 2m4 and then down to 0m3 in the channel opposite the quay at New Grimsby on Tresco. Note that a cable, marked by beacons on either side, crosses the channel just north-west of the quay. There are two hotels on the island and a small shop.

141.   A view of Cromwell's Castle, Tresco, with St. Mary's behind and Bryher with Hangman's Island on right.

If sailing in the opposite direction from St Mary's to New Grimsby leave Nut Rock to port, Hulman beacon close to starboard, Raggs beacon to port, Merrick Island close to port and thence straight to the anchorage. A useful transit between Hulman beacon and Merrick Island is to keep the latter in line with Hangman Isle, then leaving it close to port proceed as before to the anchorage. Tresco Flats dry out between Hulman beacon and the anchorage but these can be crossed by vessels up to 3m draught at HW if precisely on course. On the first occasion a stranger might be wise to treat the flats as drying 1m4.

PART TWO

PASSAGE NOTES—PRINCIPAL HEADLANDS

142. *South Foreland and lighthouse. (Photo : Aerofilms Ltd.)*   143. *Beachy Head and lighthouse from SW. (Photo : Aerofilms Ltd.)*

The following information is provided to assist in the recognition of the principal headlands coupled with brief notes on the tidal streams to be found off them. Tidal charts are not included in this book as the reader is referred to the *Admiralty Pocket Tidal Stream Atlases*. Small tidal maps can also be found in *Reed's Nautical Almanac*, together with the characters of the lighthouses. These notes are arranged from east to west.

North Foreland Conspicuous white 8-sided light tower 57m elevation on bold, nearly perpendicular chalk cliffs. At position 3.2 miles 141° from headland: north stream—0120 Dover; south-going stream +0440 Dover. Springs 2¾ knots.

South Foreland Bold irregular chalk cliff over 90m high. Two lighthouses on the summit, eastern and lower one disused. Western white square castellated tower elevation 114m; tidal streams between South Foreland and Deal. North about −0145 Dover: south about +0415 Dover, spring rate 2¼ knots.

Dungeness A low promontory with steep beach at its south-east end. Prominent lighthouse black round tower, white bands, 40m elevation. Old lighthouse and nuclear power station adjacent to west. Anchorage in roads on either side of Dungeness according to direction of wind. At position 2.4M 140° from Dungeness High lighthouse the east stream begins −0200 Dover. West stream +0430 Dover. Spring rate of about 2 knots.

Beachy Head This is a very prominent chalk headland. About a mile west of the head is a disused lighthouse, but the operative lighthouse is situated off the rocks below Beachy Head which extend seaward, and to the south-east of Beachy Head there are the rocks known as the Head Ledge extending some ½ mile from the cliffs. The lighthouse tower has a broad red band and an elevation of 31m. Seven miles east of Beachy Head are the Royal Sovereign shoals with 3m8 least water over which there are overfalls. They are marked on the southward by a prominent light tower.

Beachy Head should be given a berth of 2 miles in heavy weather as there are overfalls and rough water to the southward of it. Two miles south of the lighthouse the streams are east −0520 Dover, spring rate 2.6 knots; west +0015 Dover, spring rate 2 knots.

Selsey Bill and the Owers Selsey Bill is a low sharp point which is difficult to locate if the visibility is poor. There is a conspicuous hotel on the west side of the point. Southward of the Bill there are groups of rocks and ledges between which lie Looe channel and 7 miles south-east of Selsey Bill the Owers lighthouse buoy is moored. By keeping south of the light buoy danger is avoided but in clear weather and moderate winds the Looe channel, which is marked by buoys, affords a short cut, with the aid of a reasonably large-scale chart. Tidal streams in the Looe channel: east +0445 Dover; west −0120 Dover. Rate at springs 2.6 knots but faster between the Malt Owers and the Boulder bank. There are local variations in the directions of the streams. Three miles south of the Owers lighthouse buoy the tidal streams are west-south-west −0050 Dover; east-north-east +0540 Dover; 2½ to 3 knots at springs.

St Catherine's Point This point is at the southern extremity of the Isle of Wight and lies comparatively low at the foot of the hill which forms the highest part of the island. The lighthouse is an octagonal castellated tower standing at the back of the cliffs; it has an elevation of 41m.

There is a tide race off St Catherine's owing to the uneven bottom in strong streams. This can be very rough under wind against tide conditions and should be avoided; it is dangerous in bad weather. The turbulence of the race varies according to wind, tide and swell and is sometimes rougher or calmer than may be anticipated from the conditions. There are also

144. St. Catherine's Point.

145. Needles and Scratchell's Bay from west.

overfalls to the eastward of St Catherine's off Dunnose and a number of isolated tide rips which locally may be almost as rough as St Catherine's race. Tidal streams between St Catherine's Point and Dunnose: east +0515 Dover; west

−0015 Dover; maximum spring rate about 5 knots, weaker seaward.

The Needles Rocks   The sharp Needles rocks with the lighthouse (elevation 24m) at their seaward end are notable landmarks, but they are by no means conspicuous from a distance in hazy weather. From the west or south-west it is the high white cliffs above Scratchell's Bay, just south-east of the Needles which will first be seen, and the high down 3 miles east on which stands Tennyson's Cross. Tidal stream atlases should be referred to in the approaches to the Solent from the west as the streams are strong. The main flood stream from Durlston Head runs east-north-east towards the Needles, west of which the stream divides. The stronger flood stream runs north-east into the Needles Channel while farther south the stream runs east to south-east off the Isle of Wight coast. Conversely on the ebb the local streams join west of the Needles and set west-south-west towards Durlston Head.

In the Needles Channel streams in both directions set strongly across the Shingles. Off Hurst Point the north-east stream begins +0505 Dover and the south-west stream at −0055 Dover and attain 4 to 5 knots at springs. Off the Needles the streams tend to be earlier.

In heavy weather the western end of the Isle of Wight should be avoided if possible in strong winds, especially if from south-west when it will be worse still if late on the tide after the west-south-west stream has started. On the flood stream entry to the Solent under such conditions is safer through the North Channel which lies north of the Shingles, but in gales it is safer still to make Poole or remain in harbour.

Hengistbury Head   This headland, 5 miles east of Bournemouth pier and 1 mile south-west of the entrance of Christchurch harbour, is of local importance as it is the only headland between the Needles and Handfast Point south of Poole Bar buoy and is conspicuous from seaward. It is

146.   Hengistbury Head and breakwater from south-east.

147.   Anvil lighthouse to Durlston Point.

148.   St. Alban's Head from eastward heading for inner passage.

composed of dark reddish ironstone, but often appears of a yellowish colour from seaward; the shape is shown in the photograph. There are ledges off the headland and comparatively shoal water as far as Christchurch Ledge red can buoy, $2\frac{1}{2}$ miles south-east of it. Tidal streams are fairly strong at springs in the vicinity of the buoy, and there are overfalls on the ebb tide near the buoy and over the ledges. The streams within Christchurch Bay itself are weak.

Peveril Point to St Alban's Head There are two recognized tidal races within this area, a small but vicious one off Peveril Point and the larger race off St Alban's Head. There are also local tide rips and under certain conditions patches of rough water may be found practically the whole way from Handfast Point and Old Harry Rocks to St Alban's.

Peveril ledges extend about 3 cables from the low Peveril Point on the south side of Swanage Bay. The depths on the ledges gradually deepen seawards and the end of the reefs is marked by a RW Cheq buoy. The tidal streams set straight across the ledges which constitute a danger if a yacht is becalmed. Three cables eastward of Peveril Point the streams are north-north-east $+0500$ Dover $1\frac{1}{2}$ knots; south-south-west -0215 Dover, 3 knots. In bad weather Peveril Race extends from the Point to seaward of the buoy and especially to the south-east of it during the west-going stream. On a spring ebb tide the rate probably considerably exceeds the rates given.

Durlston Head is a rough headland of a characteristic shape shown in photograph 147, and is easily identified by the castellated building on its summit. About a mile east-south-east of the headland the north-east-going stream begins $+0530$ Dover; south-west -0030 Dover; 3 knots springs.

Inshore Eddy Between Durlston Head and extending along the Dorset coast westward beyond Lulworth there is an early eddy close inshore contrary to the main English Channel stream farther seaward. The easterly eddy starts about $+0400$ Dover quickly becoming strong and the westerly about -0200 Dover.

Anvil Head, nearly $\frac{1}{2}$ mile to the south-west of Durlston, is easily located by the conspicuous white lighthouse and white wall round its enclosure which stands above the headland.

St Alban's Head is the most southerly on this part of the coast and its shape with cliffs at the summit falling into rocks at the base is easily recognized from photograph 148. Off St Alban's Head there is a considerable tidal race which lies eastward of the head on the flood tide and westward on the ebb. The race varies considerably in its position and its severity. It extends some 3 miles seaward except during southerly winds when it lies closer inshore. It may be avoided by giving the land a berth of 3 miles. $1\frac{1}{2}$ M off the Head the easterly stream begins about $+0545$ Dover; west -0015 Dover, attaining a rate of between 4 and 5 knots at Springs. There is a passage of nearly $\frac{1}{2}$ mile between St Alban's Head and the race but it varies and may be less during onshore winds and is not entirely immune from tidal disturbance. Thus in reasonable weather vessels can avoid the worst of the overfalls by keeping inshore at St Alban's where deep water is found close to the headland. The inshore passage has the advantage of the early fair eddy but a local eddy runs down the west side of St Alban's Head to the south-east nearly continuously.

Portland Bill and Race From well seaward Portland has a characteristic shape, appearing like an island, high and broad on its northern end against the low Chesil Beach and sloping down towards the southern end. Here is situated the round tower with a red band lighthouse with an elevation of 43m.

Portland Race lies south of Portland Bill, a little to the westward during the ebb and to the eastward during the flood, where in bad weather there is confused and dangerous water so far as and over the whole of the Shambles. The worst part of

149.   Portland north-east side.

150.   Portland Bill taking the passage inside the race.

151.   Golden Cap 3 miles west of Bridport, West Bay harbour.

152.   Berry Head from the southward.

153.   Start Point and rocks from east-north-east.

154. Prawle Point and signal station from west-south-west, with Start Point in background.

155. Bolt Tail from south-west.

the Race extends nearly 2 miles from the Bill and it is well defined by the area of overfalls. At spring tides the Race sometimes attains a rate exceeding 5 to 7 knots, but these speeds are not uniform and reference is best made to the Admiralty tidal stream atlas for Approaches to Portland which shows every hourly detail. It may be added that south-west of Portland, during the west-going stream there is a northerly set into West Bay, which at times is strong. When rounding Portland Bill the navigator has two principal options to choose between. The easier one is to pass outside clear of the Race about 3 miles off the Bill or better 5 miles in bad weather especially at spring tides if the wind is against streams.

The alternative is to use the inner passage which is a channel about $\frac{1}{4}$ mile wide (varying with direction of wind) which lies between the Bill and the Race. This channel should not be used at night, and even by day only under suitable conditions, for although the water is comparatively smooth, the streams are strong and overfalls are not entirely avoided off Grove Point and west of the Bill, according to wind direction. The correct timing of the passage is a matter of the utmost importance.

When bound *westward*, round the Bill between $\frac{1}{2}$ hour before and $2\frac{1}{2}$ hours after HW Dover. When bound *eastward*, round the Bill between $4\frac{1}{2}$ hours after and 5 hours before HW Dover. Whether bound west or east through the inner passage close with Portland at least a mile to the northward of the Bill and work southwards with a fair tide to arrive off the Bill at the correct time.

Golden Cape A useful landmark $3\frac{1}{2}$ miles east of Lyme Regis and 3 miles west of Bridport. The cape rises to Golden Cap, 186m high, which has pronounced yellow cliffs at its summit which, with sun on them, may be conspicuous from a long distance even in hazy weather. Inshore streams weak.

Beer Head A conspicuous chalk cliff westward of which lie the red sandstone cliffs of Devon. Inshore streams weak,

approximately east +0600 Dover; west HW Dover.

Berry Head Bold limestone headland flat topped, with steep end falling at about 45° to the sea. White lighthouse on summit with an elevation of 58m. Coastal streams: north +0540 Dover; south −0100 Dover. $1\frac{1}{2}$ knots maximum.

Start Point A long sharp-ridged headland, with round white lighthouse, elevation 62m, which is unmistakable. There are rocks off the Start which are awash at HW and extend nearly 3 cables south of the Point. The Start race extends nearly a mile seaward of the Point, and its severity depends much on conditions of wind, tide and swell. The overfalls can be avoided in daylight by passing close to the rocks but there is an outlier on the south, so care is needed. It is simpler to give the Point a berth of at least a mile. Three miles southward of the Point the streams are: east-north-east +0455 Dover; west-south-west −0120 Dover, about 2 knots Springs. Off Start rocks the streams are about an hour earlier and attain about 4 knots at Springs but are irregular at Neaps.

Prawle Point This Point lies $3\frac{1}{2}$ miles west of Start Point on the south-east side of the Salcombe indentation and has a Coastguard Station at its summit.

Bolt Head and Bolt Tail Bolt Head stands on the west side of the entrance to Salcombe. The ridge of dark rugged cliffs extending to Bolt Tail is conspicuous.

Rame Head is conspicuous when one is approaching Plymouth Sound.

Dodman Point is a most conspicuous headland standing about halfway between Fowey and Falmouth. It is precipitous, 110m high, with a stone cross near south-west extremity. Irregular bottom and tide rips $1\frac{1}{2}$ miles seaward.

Lizard Point The Lizard is a bold headland with conspicuous white buildings and a white wall round their enclosure which stand near its summit. The octagonal tower of the white lighthouse (elevation 70m) is situated at the eastern

156.   *Bolt Head from south-east with Starhole Bay just showing on right.*

157.   *Rame Head from south-east.*

158.   Dodman Point and stone cross at summit from south-east.

159.   St. Anthony Head on east side of entrance to Falmouth.

160. Lizard Point. (Photo : Aerofilms Ltd.)

end of the buildings. Six cables to eastward there is a coastguard station and Lloyd's signal station, which is in almost continuous use with passing ships making their landfalls and departures.

The group of rocks known as Stag Rocks, some of which are above water and others dry 4 to 5 m, extend over ½ mile south of the Lizard. These can be seen at most states of the tide and avoided, but a mile east of Lizard Point lie the Vrogue Rocks off Bass Point which have less than 2m over them at LW. The Craggan Rocks, with 1m5 over them, lie north-east of Bass Point, but these dangers will be avoided by vessels proceeding east or west to the southward of the Stag Rocks. The Lizard Race extends 2 to 3 miles seaward of the Stag Rocks, and at times there is a race south-east of the head. The state of the seas varies considerably according to hour of tide and wind direction, and the seas may be very rough with strong westerly winds against the down channel stream. Under suitable conditions pass outside the Stag Rocks where the streams start east +0145 Dover; west −0345 Dover. Spring rates are 2 and 3 knots respectively and at times stronger. In rough weather or when a swell is running, especially with wind against a spring tide vessels should keep 3 or more miles off Lizard Point.

Note that the Lizard is the most westerly of the conspicuous headlands on the south coast of England. It is a dividing line in the sense that west of it there is only limited shelter in Penzance Bay but eastward there are many harbours available in bad weather.

HARBOUR PLANS

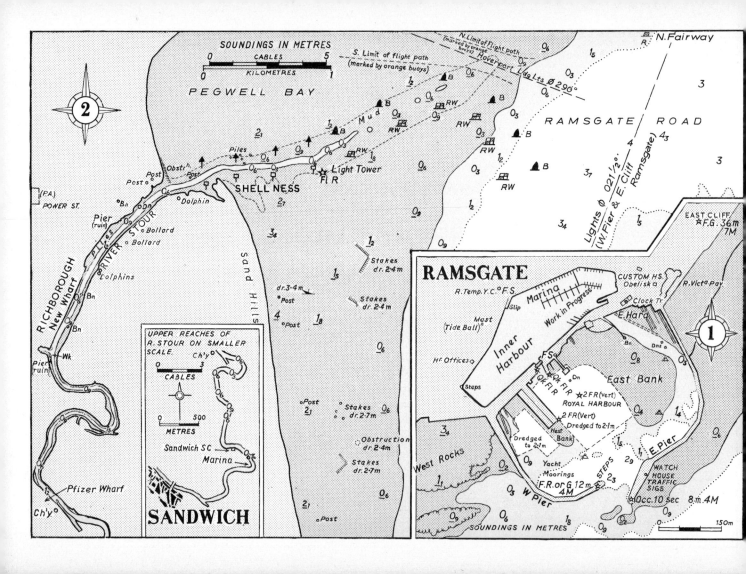

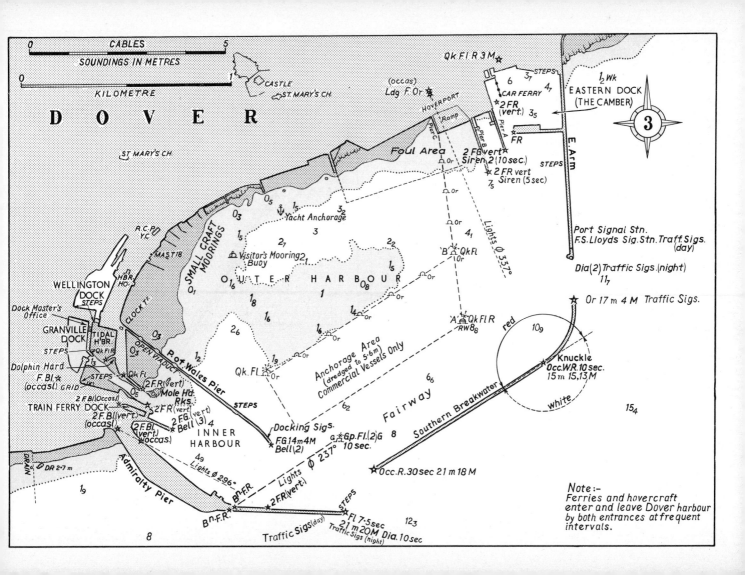

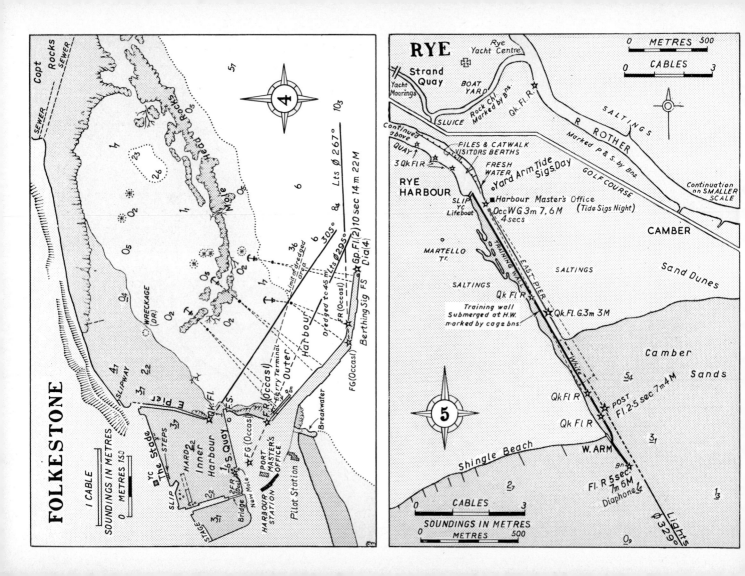

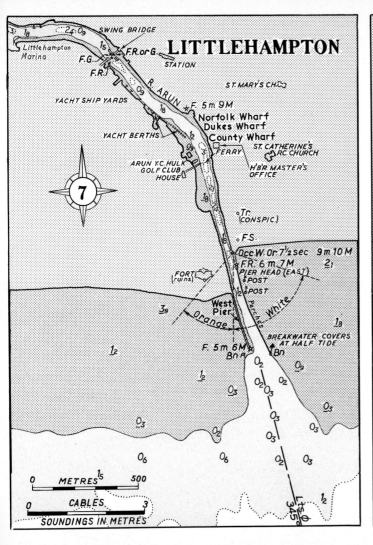
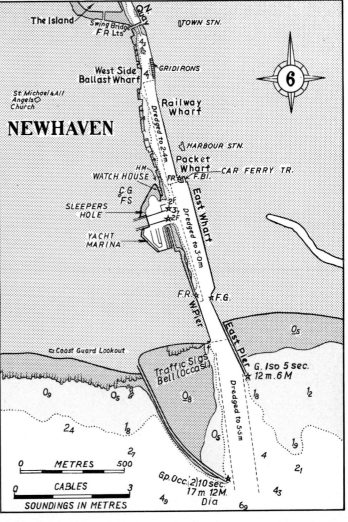

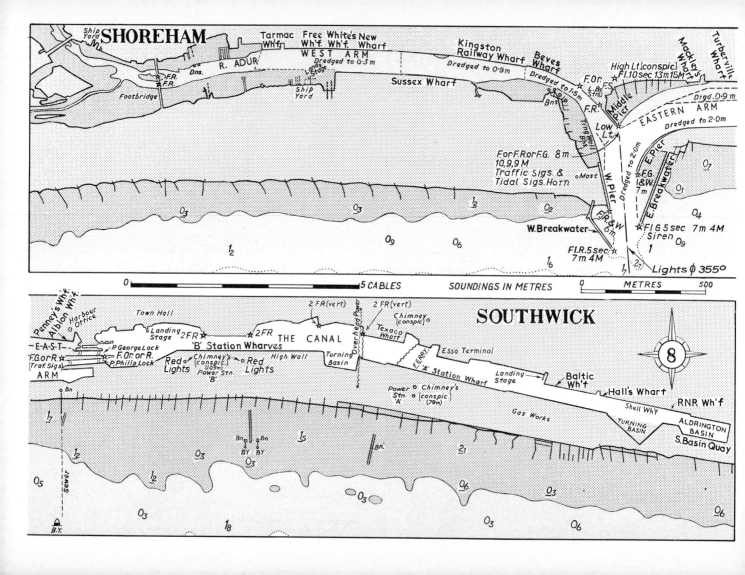

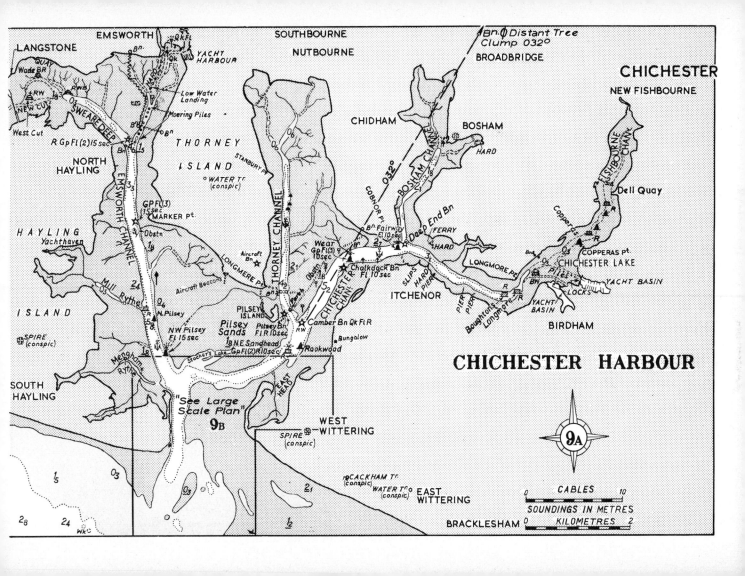

CHICHESTER HARBOUR

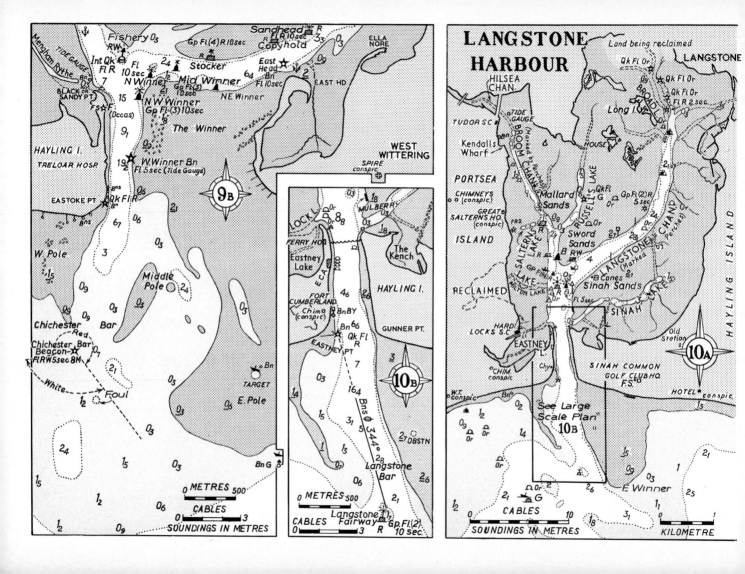

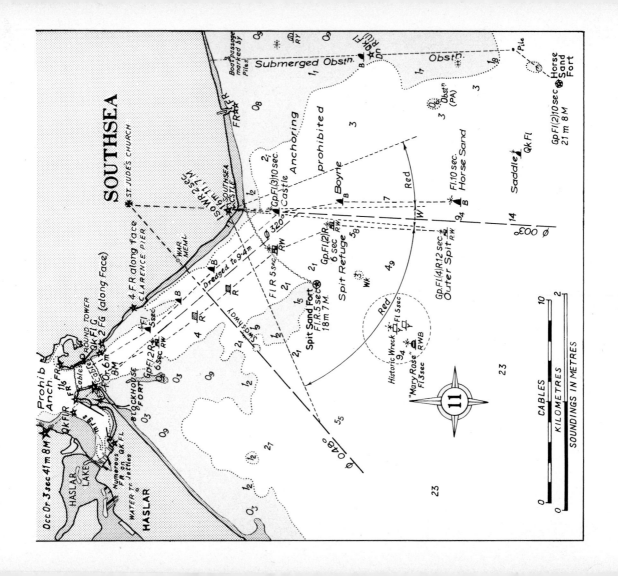

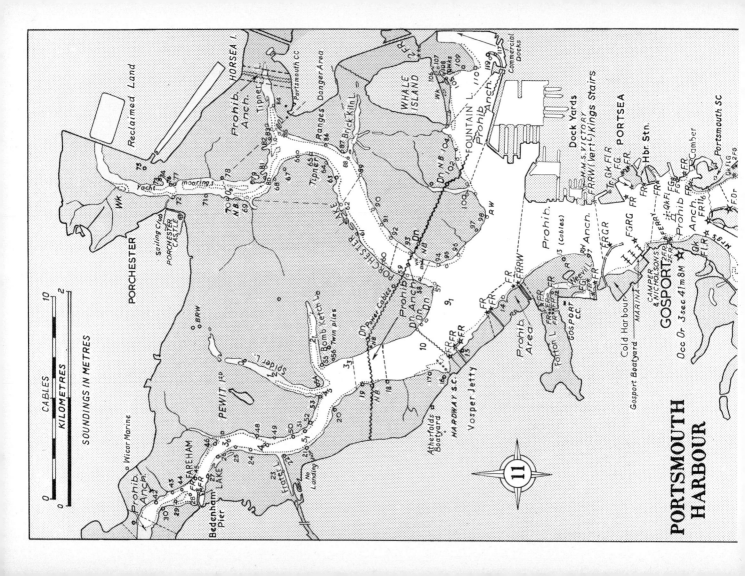

PORTSMOUTH
HARBOUR

11

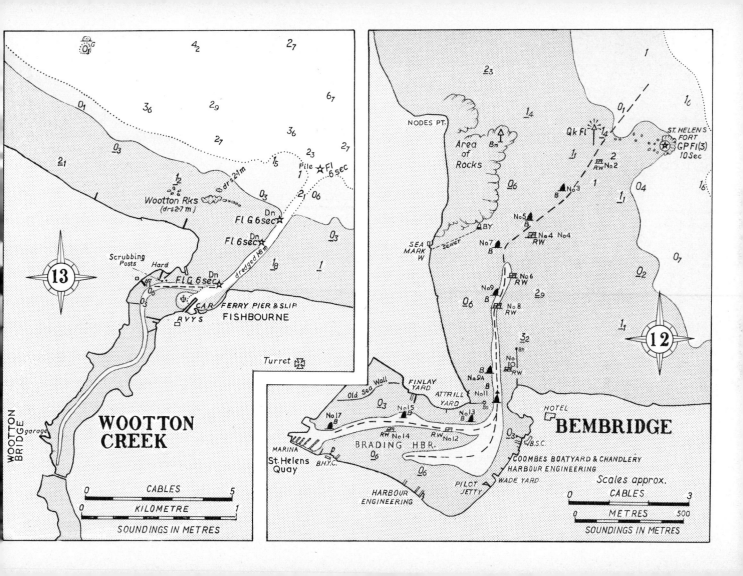

WOOTTON CREEK

13

WOOTTON BRIDGE

garage

Wootton Rks
(drs 2·7 m)

Fl G 6 sec
Fl 6 sec
Fl G 6 sec

Scrubbing Posts
Hard
dredged 18 m

CAR FERRY PIER & SLIP
R.VY.S
FISHBOURNE

Turret

Pile ★ Fl 6 sec

drs 2·1 m

| CABLES | 5 |
| KILOMETRE | 1 |

SOUNDINGS IN METRES

BEMBRIDGE

12

NODES PT.

Area of Rocks
Bn

SEA MARK W

Sewer

St. HELENS FORT
G P Fl (3) 10 Sec

Qk Fl

RW No 2
B No 3
No 5 B
No 7 B
No 9 B
No 11 B
No 13 B

RW No 4 No 4
RW No 6
RW No 8
No 10 RW
No 9A B

ATTRILL YARD

FINLAY YARD

Old Sea Wall

No 17 B
No 15 B
RW No 14
RW No 12

BRADING HBR.

MARINA
St. Helens Quay

B.H.Y.C.

HARBOUR ENGINEERING

PILOT JETTY

WADE YARD

B.S.C.

HOTEL

COOMBES BOATYARD & CHANDLERY
HARBOUR ENGINEERING

Scales approx.

| CABLES | 3 |
| METRES | 500 |

SOUNDINGS IN METRES

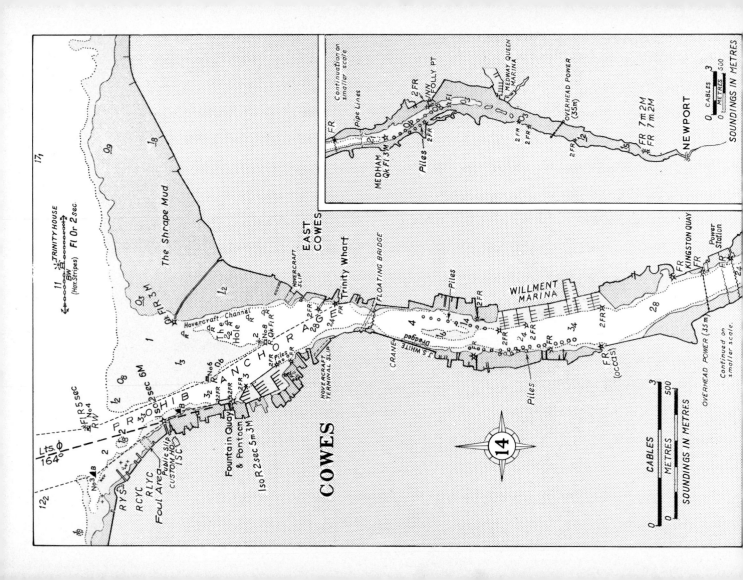

COWES

EAST COWES

The Shrape Mud

TRINITY HOUSE
B. W. (Hor. Stripes) Fl Or 2 sec.

Qk Fl R 3 M

The Hovercraft Channel
Hole

HOVERCRAFT SLIP
Trinity Wharf
FLOATING BRIDGE

Piles
2FR

WILLMENT MARINA

28G
24
Qk Fl R

Fl R 5 sec
No4
R W

Lts.
164°

No3 B

RYS
RCYC
RLYC
Foul Area
Public Slip
CUSTOM HO.
ISC

Fountain Quay
& Pontoon
Iso R 2 sec 5m 3M

Iso G Fl 3 sec

Piles
No.5 & 6

2FR
2FR

HOVERCRAFT TERMINAL SLIP

CRANE
J.S WHITE Dredged

Piles

FR
(occas)

KINGSTON QUAY
FR
Power Station
Fl G.
OVERHEAD POWER (35m)
Continued on smaller scale.

14

CABLES 3
METRES 500
SOUNDINGS IN METRES

SHIP RANCHORAGE

NEWPORT

Continuation on smaller scale.
Pipe Lines
MEDHAM
Qk Fl 3 M
Piles
POLLY PT
2FR
MEDWAY QUEEN
MEDWAY QUEEN MARINA
OVERHEAD POWER (35m)
FR 7m 2M
FR 7m 2M

0 CABLES 3
0 METRES 500
SOUNDINGS IN METRES

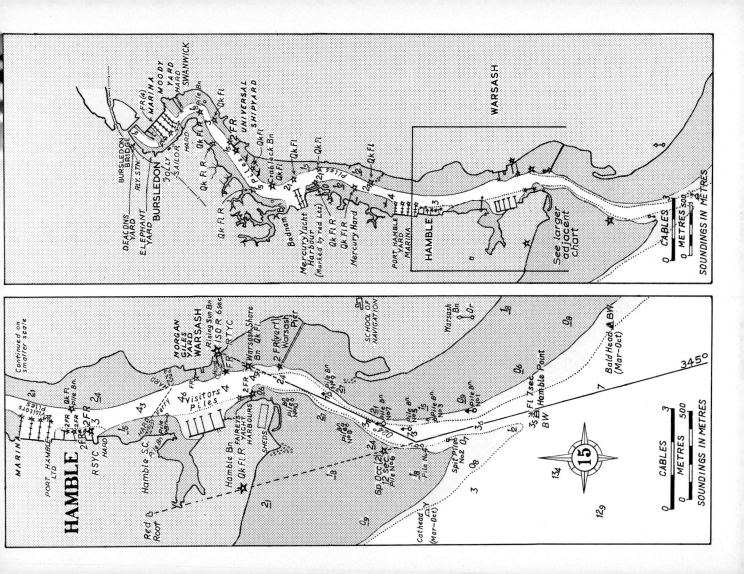

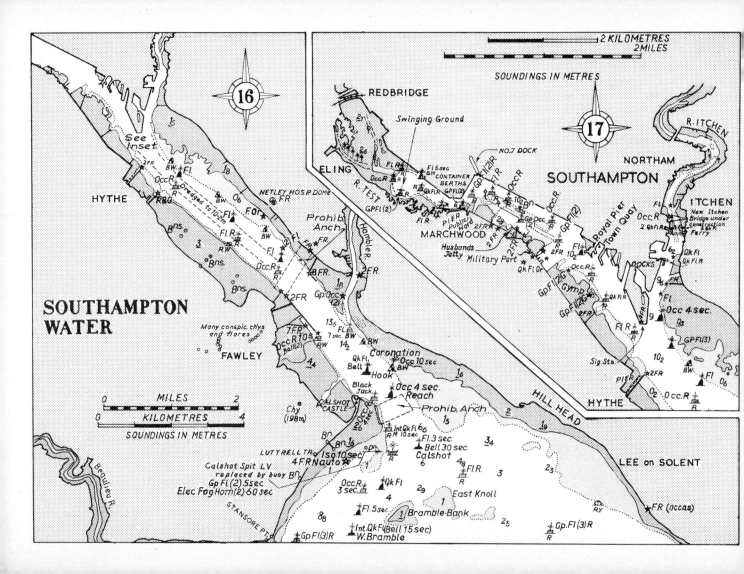

SOUTHAMPTON WATER

16

HYTHE

See Inset

2FR
BW Fl
OccR
R&G
BW
O₆
Dredged to 10·2ᵐ
BW Fl
FOr
BNs
BW Fl
FI.R
RW
BNs
3
BNs

NETLEY HOSP. DOME
FR
Prohib. Anch.
Hamble R.
8.FR.
F.R.
2FR
Gp.Occ (2)
1₈

13₆
Fl.7sec.BW
7FR
OccR 10s
Bell(2)
RW
14₂
BW
4₄
QkFl
Bell
BW
Hook
Coronation Occ 10 sec
BW
Black Jack
Occ 4 sec. Reach
Prohib. Anch
1₅

FAWLEY

Many conspic. chys and flares

Chy (198ᵐ)
CALSHOT CASTLE
BN
BN 1₆
Iso 10 sec
LUTTRELL TR₉
4.F.R.Nauto
Calshot Spit L.V.
replaced by buoy BN
GpFl(2)5sec
Elec Fog Horn(2) 60 sec

STANSORE PT.

Beaulieu R.

MILES   2
KILOMETRES   4
SOUNDINGS IN METRES

8₈
Int.QkFl (Bell 15 sec)
W.Bramble
GpFl(3)R

1₅
OccR 3 sec.
QkFl
4
Bramble Bank
1
2₉
East Knoll
2₅
GpFl(3)R

Int.QkFl
RR 10 sec
Fl.3 sec
Bell 30 sec
Calshot
6
3₄
4₈ FI.R
3
2₃
1₉

17

SOUNDINGS IN METRES

2 KILOMETRES
2 MILES

REDBRIDGE

Swinging Ground

ELING

R. TEST

FI.R
OccR
GPFl(2)
NO.7 DOCK
Fl.5sec.BW
CONTAINER BERTHS
QkFl.R GPFl(2)
GpFl(2)R
FR
OccR
BN
10₂
OccR
PIER
Public Hard
FI.R
GPF(2)
2FR
MARCHWOOD
Husbands Jetty
Military Part
QkFl.Dr
2FR
10₂

NORTHAM
SOUTHAMPTON
R.ITCHEN

Occ R
New Itchen Bridge under construction
FI.R
2 QkFl.R
Ferry
QkFl
QkFl.R
DOCKS
Royal Pier
Town Quay
Gp.F(2)
2G
Gymp
GpF(2)G
QkF.R R
FI.R
Fl Occ 4 sec.
9₅
GPFl(3)
10₂
Sig.Sta.
PIER
2FR
BW
FI. O₆
HYTHE
O₂ Occ R
R

HILL HEAD

LEE on SOLENT

R.Y.
FR (occas)

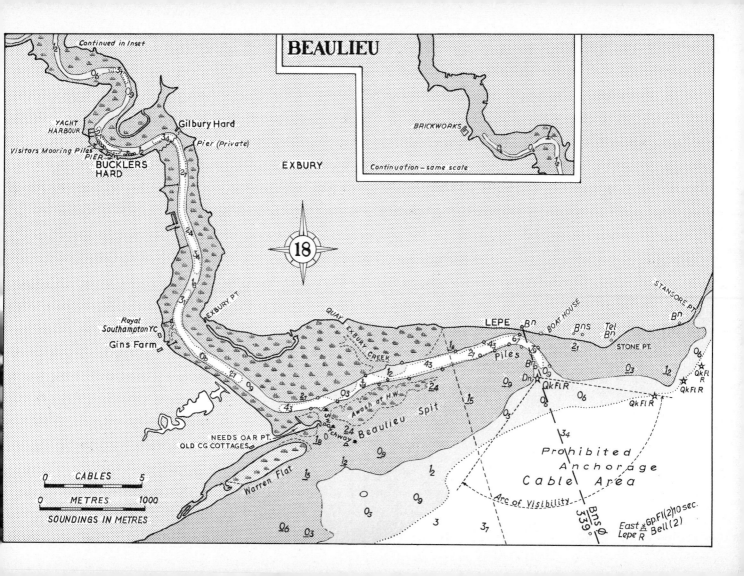

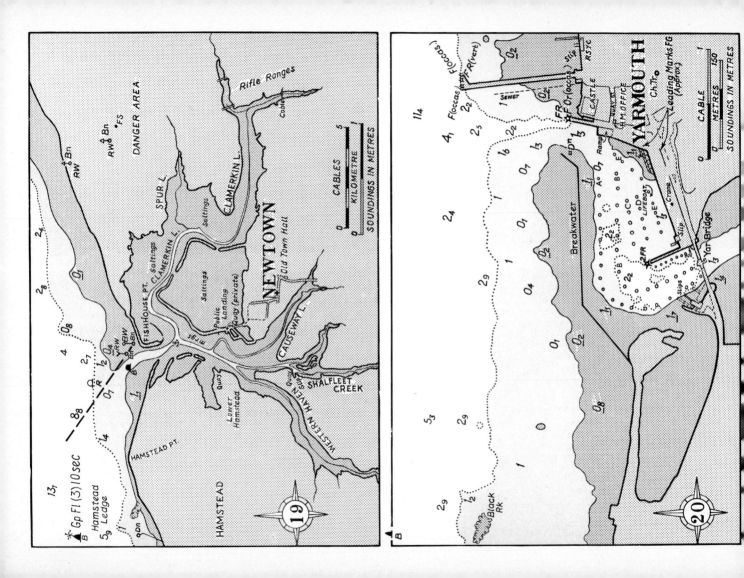

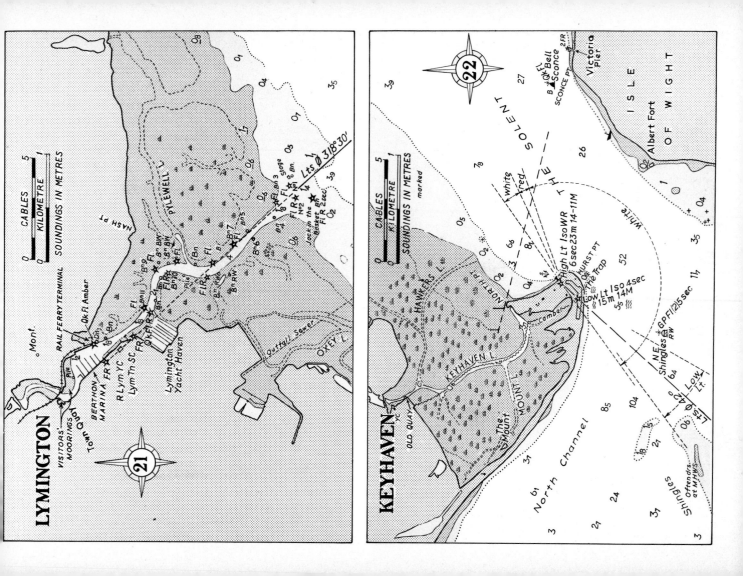

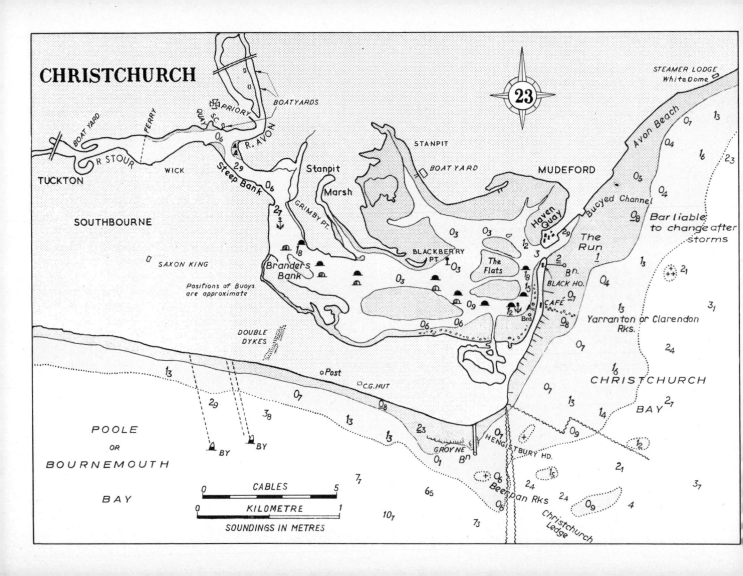

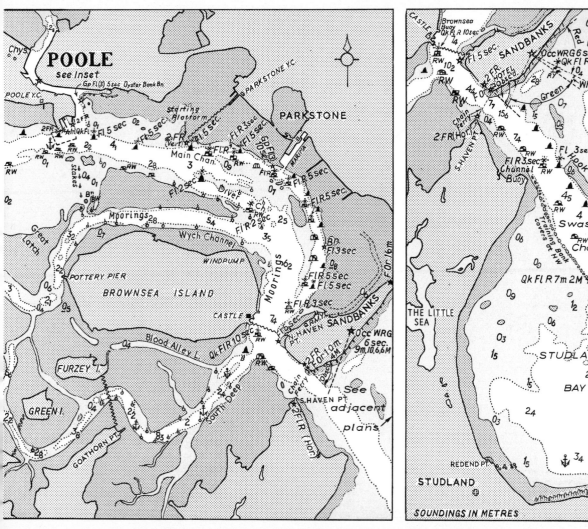

POOLE
see Inset

Gp Fl(3) 5sec Oyster Bank Bn

Chys

POOLE Y.C.

PARKSTONE Y.C.

PARKSTONE

2FR

AlnQkFl

Fl 5 sec

RW

RW

RW

stakes

RW

Starting Platform

Main Chan.

3

2 FR (Vert)

Fl 5 sec

Fl 5 sec

Fl R 5 sec

Fl R 5 sec

Gp Fl(3) 10 sec

MARINA

Fl R 5 sec

Fl R 5 sec

Fl 2 sec

Diver

Ch RW

Fl R 2

Bn BW

Moorings

Wych Channel

54

25

35

Bn Fl 3 sec

Fl R 2

Geat Latch

WINDPUMP

Moorings 62

Fl R 5 sec

Fl 5 sec

POTTERY PIER

BROWNSEA ISLAND

F Or 6m

Fl R 3 sec

Fl R 3 sec

CASTLE

N. HAVEN PT.

SANDBANKS

Blood Alley L.

Qk Fl R 10 sec

RW

Occ WRG 6 sec
9m 10,6,6M

2FR F Or 10m

FURZEY I.

GREEN I.

S.HAVEN PT.

South Deep

Chain Ferry

GOATHORN PT.

2 FR (Hor)

See adjacent plans

SOUTH-DEEP

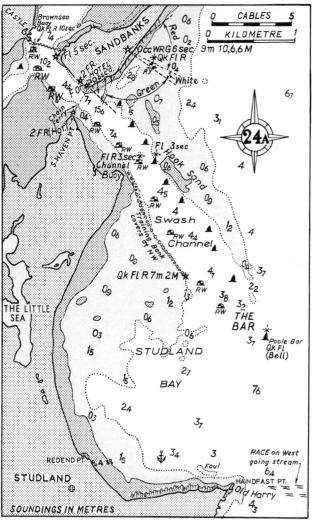

CABLES 0 — 5

KILOMETRE 0 — 1

CASTLE

Brownsea Buoy
Qk Fl R 10 sec

SANDBANKS

Red

Fl 5 sec

2 FR HOTEL

Occ WRG 6 sec
9m 10,6,6M

Qk Fl R

Green

White

RW 102

RW

RW

2 FR (Hor)

Chain Ferry

S. HAVEN PT.

RW

Fl R 3 sec
Channel Buoy

Fl Hook Sand

Fl 3 sec

Qk Fl R

RW

RW

RW

Swash

Channel

RW

THE LITTLE SEA

Qk Fl R 7m 2M

RW

RW

THE BAR

Poole Bar
Qk Fl
(Bell)

STUDLAND BAY

REDEND PT.

STUDLAND

RACE on West going stream

HANDFAST PT.

Old Harry

SOUNDINGS IN METRES

24A

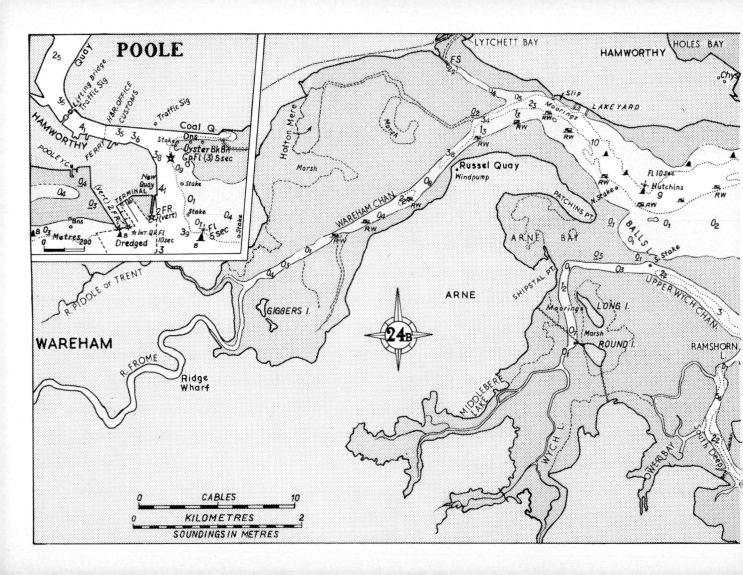

POOLE

QUAY

2.5

Lifting bridge Traffic Sig

3.5

HBR. OFFICE CUSTOMS

Traffic Sig

HAMWORTHY

FERRY

4.1

3.5 3.6

Coal Q.

Dns

Stake

Oyster Bk Bn
Gp Fl (3) 5 sec

3.8

0.9

POOLE Y.C.

0.4

0.4

New Quay

4.1

Stake

0.3

TERMINAL

2 FR (vert)

2 FR (vert)

Stake

0.1

0.4

Int. Q.R. Fl 10sec

Stake

Fl 5 sec

3.9

B

Bns

B 0.3

Metres

200

Dredged

0.3

HAMWORTHY

LYTCHETT BAY

HOLES BAY

HAMWORTHY

Chy

FS

2.2

0.4

0.5

Slip

Moorings

RWO

LAKEYARD

3.4

1.3

RW

2.3

RW

1.3

RW

RW

10

3.8

RW

N Stake

FL 10sec

Hutchins

9

RW

RW

0.1

0.1

0.1

BALLS L.S. Stake

PATCHINS PT.

0.3

0.1

2.2

Russel Quay

Windpump

0.8

WAREHAM CHAN

RW

0.4

RW

0.1

0.3

0.4

RW

0.3

UPPER WYCH CHAN.

3

0.3

0.1

ARNE   BAY

SHIPSTAL PT.

1.2

Moorings

LONG I.

RAMSHORN L.

R. PIDDLE or TRENT

Marsh

Holton Mere

Marsh

GIGGERS I.

WAREHAM

R. FROME

Ridge Wharf

24 B

ARNE

0.1

Marsh

ROUND I.

WYCH L.

MIDDLEBERE LAKE

OWERLBAY

SOUTH DEEP

2.2

CABLES   10

0   KILOMETRES   2

SOUNDINGS IN METRES

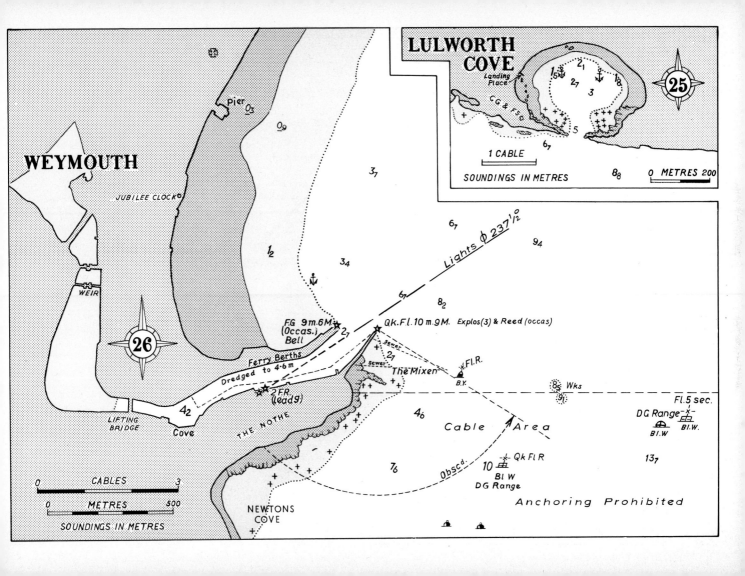

LULWORTH COVE

Landing Place

C.G. & F.S.

1 CABLE

SOUNDINGS IN METRES

0 METRES 200

25

WEYMOUTH

Pier

JUBILEE CLOCK

WEIR

26

LIFTING BRIDGE

Cove

THE NOTHE

NEWTONS COVE

CABLES

0 ——————————— 3

0 ——————————— 500

METRES

SOUNDINGS IN METRES

F.G 9m.6M.
(Occas.)
Bell

Ferry Berths
Dredged to 4·6 m

2 F.R.
(lead g)

Qk.Fl. 10 m.9M.   Explos(3) & Reed (occas)

Lights ⌀ 237½°

The Mixen

sewer

sewer

Fl.R.

B.Y.

Wks

Cable   Area

Obscd.

Qk Fl R

Bl W
DG Range

Anchoring   Prohibited

Fl.5 sec.

DG Range

Bl W.

Bl.W.

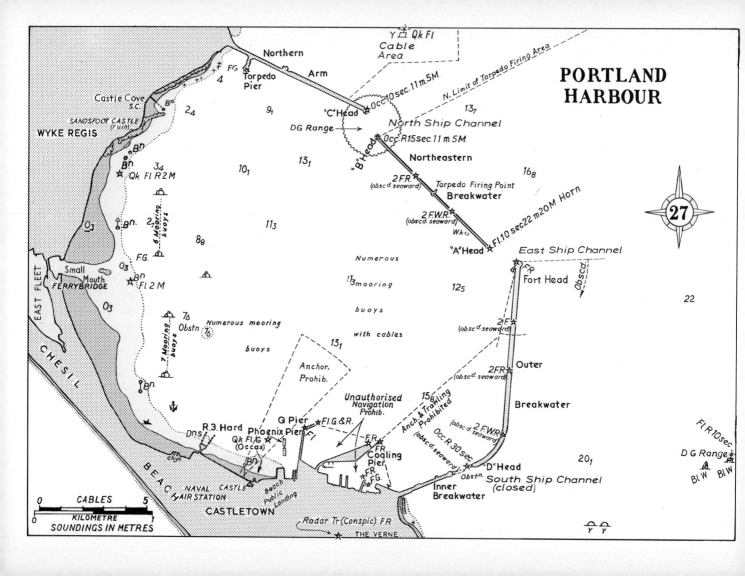

PORTLAND HARBOUR

Y ⌂ Qk Fl
Cable
Area

Northern

Arm

N. Limit of Torpedo Firing Area

FG
Torpedo
Pier
4

Castle Cove
S.C.

Sandsfoot Castle
(ruin)

WYKE REGIS

Bn.

2₄

9₁

"C" Head

Occ.10 sec.11 m.5M.

North Ship Channel

13₇

DG Range

Occ.R.15 sec.11 m.5M.

"B" Head

Northeastern

Bn.

3₄
Qk Fl R 2M

10₁

13₁

2 FR
(obscd. seaward)

Torpedo Firing Point
Breakwater

16₈

Bn.

6 Mooring buoys

2 mooring buoys

11₃

8₈

2 FWR.
(obscd. seaward)

Wk ○

Fl.10 sec.22 m.20M. Horn

O₃

Bn.

"A" Head

East Ship Channel

Small
Mouth
FERRYBRIDGE

F.G.

O₃

Bn.
Fl 2M

Numerous

11₃ mooring

12₅

FR

Fort Head

Obscd.

22

O₃

Obstn.
7₆

Numerous mooring

buoys

2 F
(obscd. seaward)

7 Mooring buoys

buoys

with cables

13₁

2 FR
(obscd. seaward)

Outer

Bn.

Anchor.
Prohib.

Breakwater

Unauthorised
Navigation
Prohib.

15₈ Anch. & Trawling Prohibited

Dns.
R.3. Hard

Q Pier

F.I.G.&R.

2 FWR.
(obscd. seaward)

Phoenix Pier

Qk Fl./G
(Occas)

Fl

FR
FR

Occ R 30 sec

2 FWR.
(obscd. seaward)

Bn.

Coaling
Pier

FR

Obstn.

"D" Head
South Ship Channel
(closed)

Fl R 10 sec.

F.G.

D G Range

NAVAL
AIR STATION

Beach Public Landing

CASTLE

Inner
Breakwater

20₁

Bl.W   Bl.W

CASTLETOWN

Radar Tr (Conspic) FR

THE VERNE

Y Y

CABLES
0   5

KILOMETRE
0   1
SOUNDINGS IN METRES

27

CHESIL
BEACH
EAST FLEET

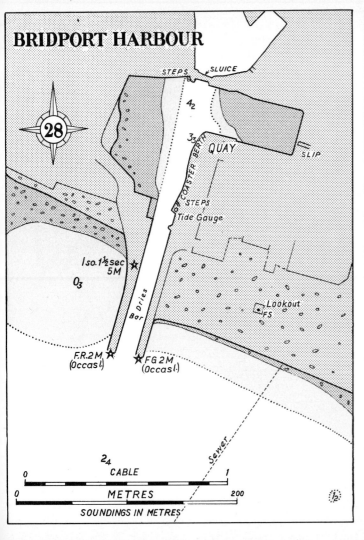

BRIDPORT HARBOUR

28

STEPS   SLUICE

4₂

3₅

COASTER BERTH

QUAY

SLIP

STEPS

Tide Gauge

Iso. 1½ sec 5M

0₃

Dries

Bar

Lookout
FS

F.R.2M (Occasl.)

FG 2M (Occasl.)

Sewer

2₄

CABLE
0   1

METRES
0   200

SOUNDINGS IN METRES

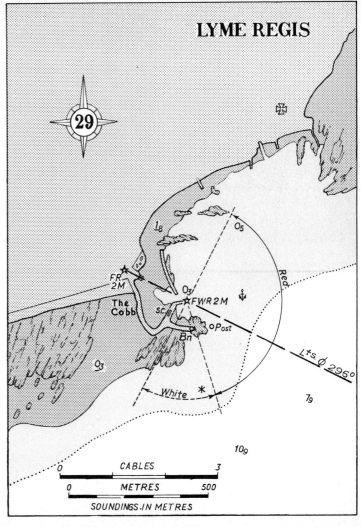

LYME REGIS

29

1₈

0₅

FR. 2M

The Cobb

O₃

FWR 2M

SC.

Bn

Post

Red

Lts ◊ 295°

0₃

White   *

7₉

10₉

CABLES
0   3

METRES
0   500

SOUNDINGS IN METRES

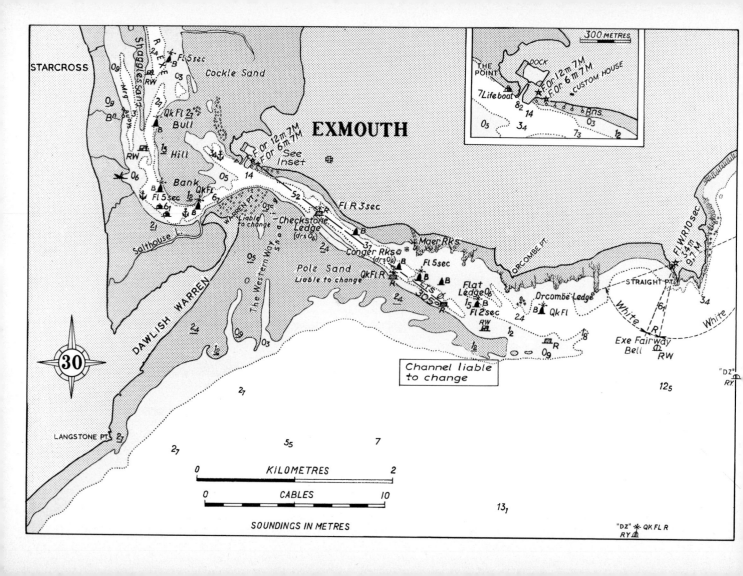

STARCROSS

Shaggles sand

Cockle Sand

EXMOUTH

Fl 5sec

RW

Qk Fl 2

Bull

Hill

Bank

Fl 5sec

QkFl

Salthouse

WARREN PT.

Liable
to change

Checkstone
Ledge
(drs 0·6)

Conger Rks
(dr 3·0)

Pole Sand
Liable to change

QkFl R

F.Or 12m 7M
F.Or 6m 7M

See
Inset

Fl.R 3sec

Maer Rks

Fl 5sec

Flat
Ledge

Fl 2sec

RW

The Western Way

DAWLISH WARREN

ORCOMBE PT.

Orcombe Ledge

Qk Fl

Channel liable
to change

STRAIGHT PT.

FlWR10 sec
3·4m
9·7 M

White   R

White

Exe Fairway
Bell
RW

"DZ"
RY

LANGSTONE PT.

KILOMETRES

CABLES

SOUNDINGS IN METRES

"DZ"   QK FL R
RY

Inset:

THE
POINT

DOCK

F.Or 12m 7M
F.Or 6m 7M

CUSTOM HOUSE

Lifeboat

Bns.

300 METRES

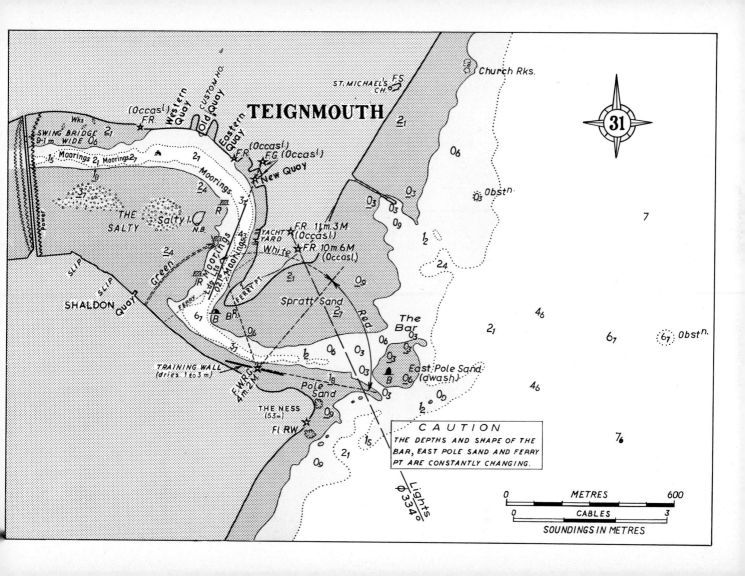

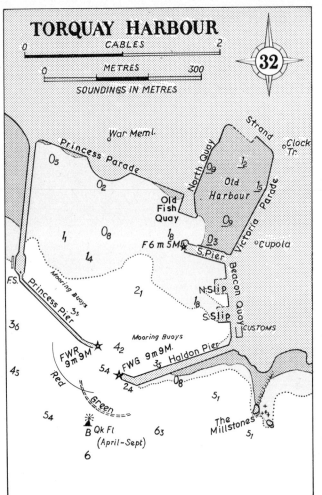

TORQUAY HARBOUR

CABLES
0   2

METRES
0   300

SOUNDINGS IN METRES

32

War Meml.

Strand

Clock Tr.

Princess Parade

0_5

0_2

North Quay

0_9

1_2

Old Harbour

1_5

Old Fish Quay

Victoria Parade

0_9

Cupola

1_1

0_8

1_8

0_3

F 6 m 5M

1_4

S. Pier

Beacon Quay

2_1

N. Slip

1_8

S. Slip

CUSTOMS

F.S.

Mooring buoys

Princess Pier

3_5

Mooring Buoys

3_6

FWR 9m 9M

4_2

FWG 9m 9M.

Haldon Pier

3_5

0_8

4_5

Red

5_4

2_4

Green

5_1

The Millstones

5_1

5_4

B Qk Fl
(April–Sept)

6_3

6

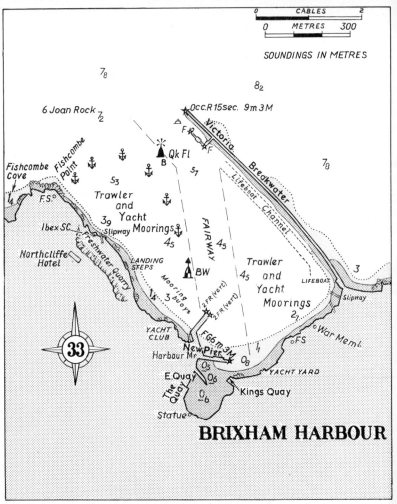

CABLES
0   2

METRES
0   300

SOUNDINGS IN METRES

7_8

8_2

6 Joan Rock 7_2

Occ.R 15sec. 9m 3M

F

Victoria

7_8

Fishcombe Cove

Fishcombe Point

Qk Fl

B

5_7

F

Breakwater

5_3

Lifeboat Channel

F.S.

1_4

Trawler and Yacht Moorings

3_9

4_5

FAIRWAY

4_5

Ibex SC

Slipway

4_5

3

Northcliffe Hotel

Freshwater Quay

LANDING STEPS

BW

Trawler and Yacht Moorings

1_4

Mooring buoys

3_5

4_5

LIFEBOAT

Slipway

2 FR(vert)

2_1

War Meml.

YACHT CLUB

2 FR(vert)

F.S.

New Pier

FG6m3M

0_8

YACHT YARD

Harbour Mr.

1_1

E.Quay

0_5

0_6

Kings Quay

The Quay

0_6

Statue

BRIXHAM HARBOUR

33

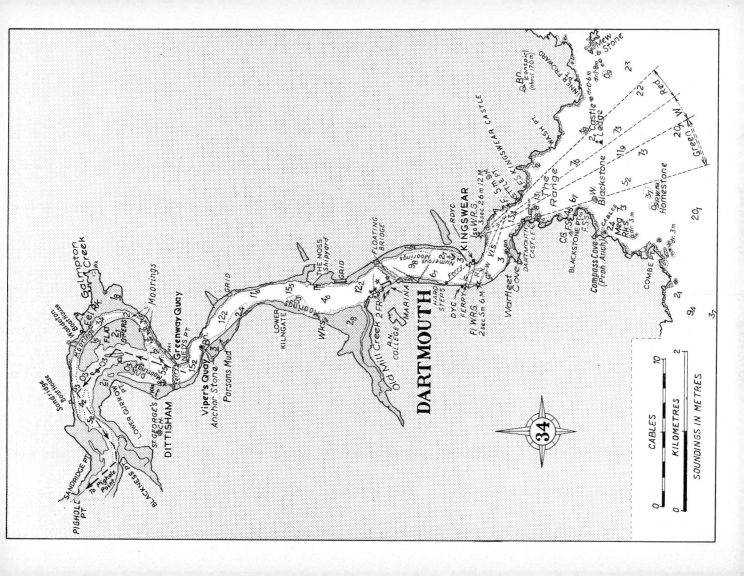

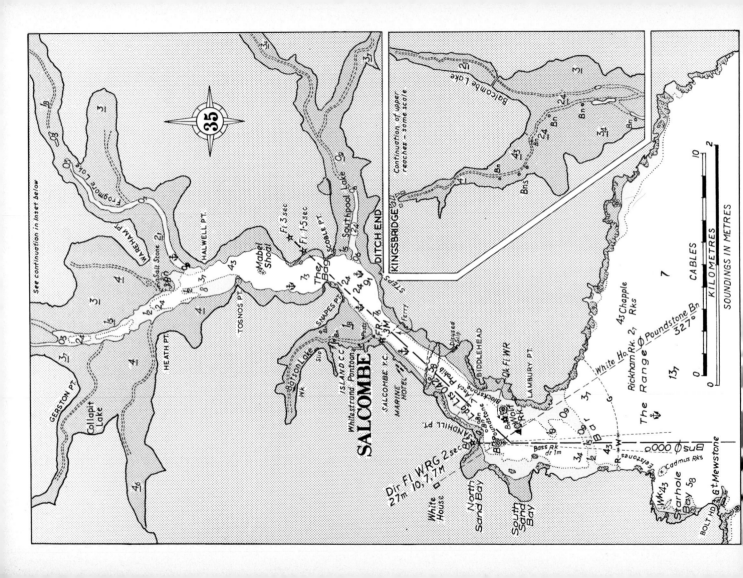

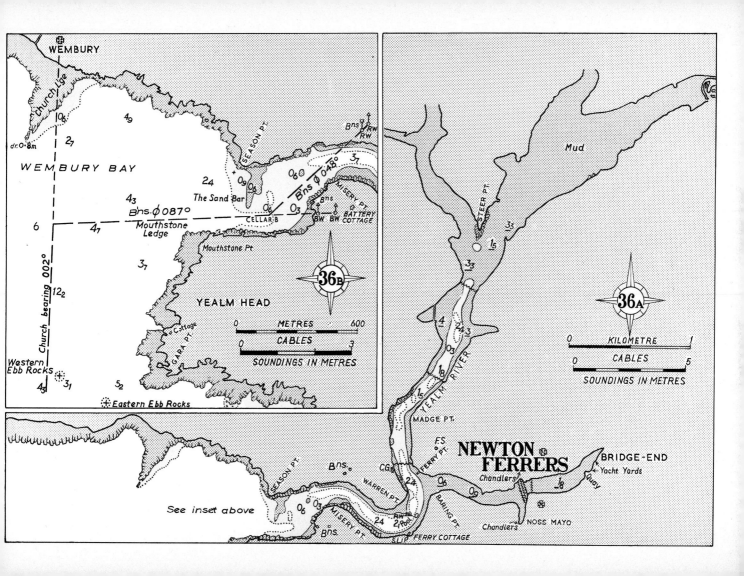

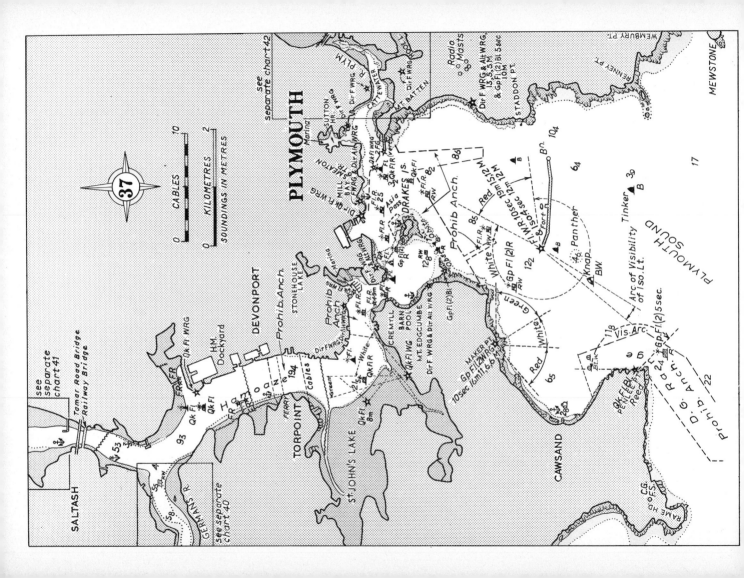

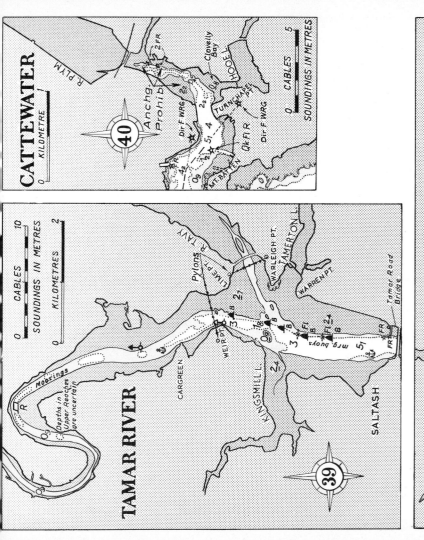

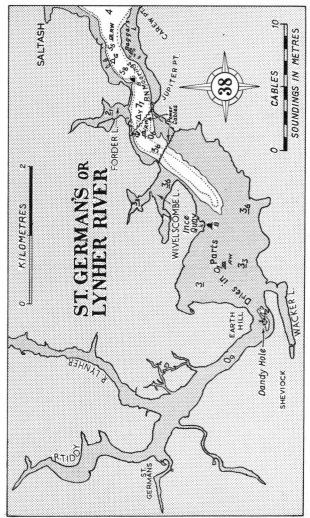

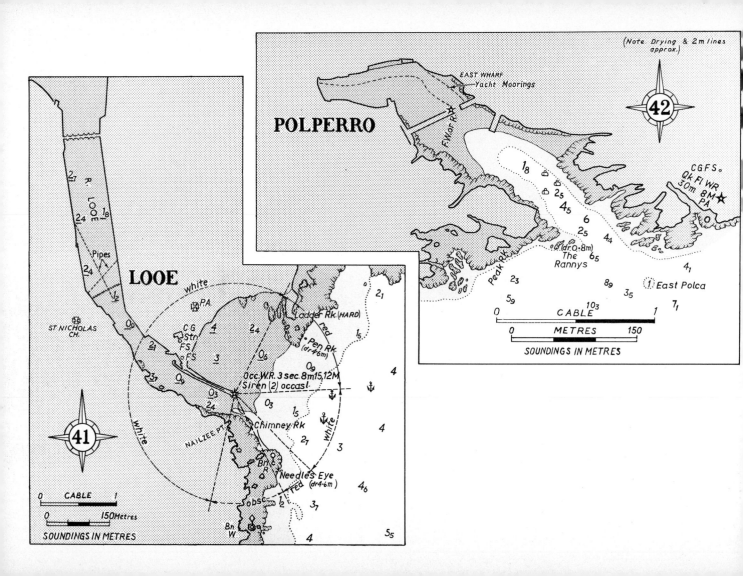

POLPERRO

(Note. Drying & 2 m lines approx.)

EAST WHARF
Yacht Moorings

F.W.or R.

42

CGFS.
Qk Fl WR
30m 8M ★
PA

1₈
2₅
4₅
6
2₅
4₄
4₁
(dr.0·8m)
The
Rannys
6₅
1 East Polca
Peak Rk.
2₃
8₉
3₅
7₁
5₉
10₃
CABLE

0   CABLE   1
0   METRES   150
SOUNDINGS IN METRES

R. LOOE

2₇
1₈
2₄
Pipes
2₄
½
St NICHOLAS CH.
0₆
2₄
2₇
0₉
0₃
2₄

LOOE

white
P.A.
C.G. Stn
FS
FS
4
3
2₄
0₆
Ladder Rk. (HARD)
red
Pen Rk. (dr.4·6m)
0₉
white
2₁
1₅

Occ.W.R. 3 sec. 8m15,12M
Siren (2) occasl
0₃
1₅
Chimney Rk
2₇
red
Needles Eye (dr.4·6m)
Bn R
obsc
2
Bn W
0₉

NAILZEE PT.

41

white

4
4
4
3
4₆
3₇
5₅
4

0   CABLE   1
0   150 Metres
SOUNDINGS IN METRES

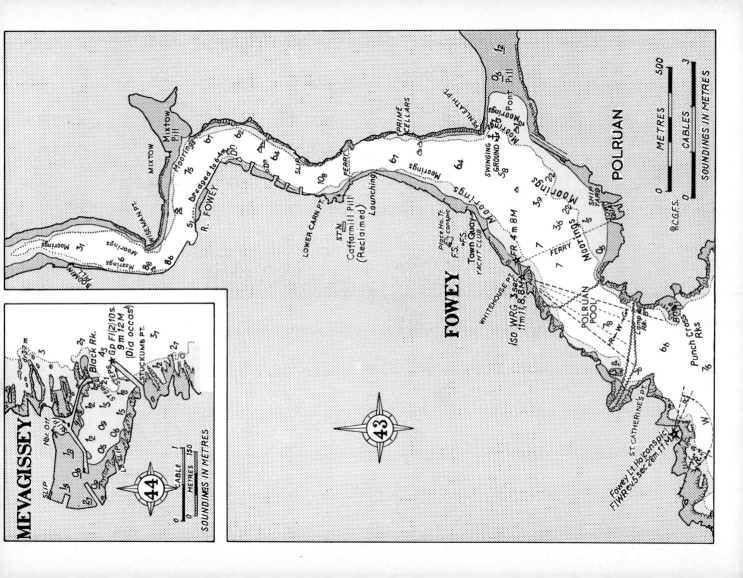

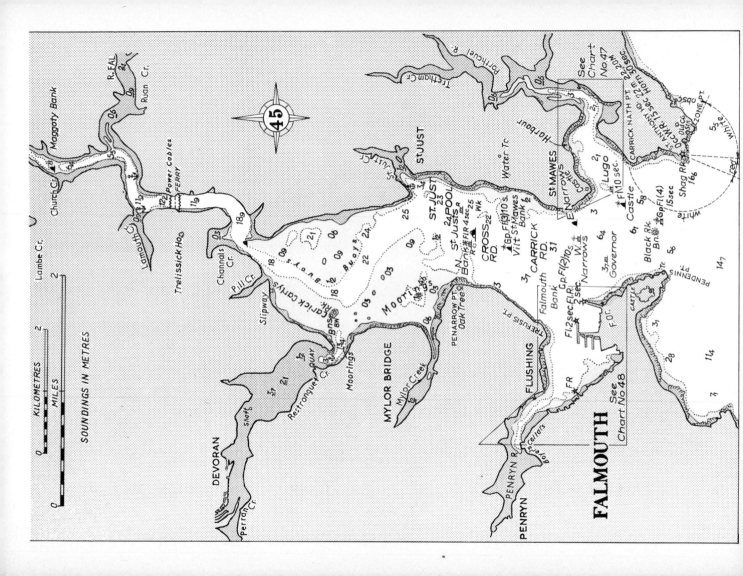

FALMOUTH
See Chart No 48

45

SOUNDINGS IN METRES

KILOMETRES

MILES

R. FAL

Ruan Cr.

Church Cr.

Maggoty Bank

Lambe Cr.

Power Cables

FERRY

Thelissick Hoo

Lamouth Cr.

Channals Cr.

Pill Cr.

Carrick Carlys

Slipway

Bsn

BW

Restrongnet Cr.

Moorings

Shaft

Perran Cr.

DEVORAN

PENRYN

MYLOR BRIDGE

Mylo Creek

Penarrow Pt.

Oak Trees

Trefusis Pt.

FLUSHING

Penryn R.

Cellars

Bolo

FR

FR

F.O.C.

Fl.2 sec.F.I.R.
2 sec.

Falmouth Bank Gp.Fl(2)10 s.
W.

CARRICK RD.
31

3 m
Governor

6 4

Narrows

Pendennis Pt.

Castle

Black Rk.
Bn.

7

11 4

14 7

2 8

3 1

St Just's Bank 2

Vilt St Mawes

CROSS RD.

Gp.Fl(3)10 s.

St Just's Bank
R Cs.

St JUST'S POOL
23

24

N. Bank
FI.R 4 sec.

Wk

Mooti

B.u.o.y.s

Carrick Rk.

18 9

0 3

0 3

0 6

18

2 1

0 6

0 9

25

0 9

0 9

22

0 3

24

21

12

18

0 3

0 3

0 6

17 48

0 9

St JUST CHURCH

St JUST

St MAWES

E Narrow's

E Narrow's

Lugo
Fl.10 sec.

Castle
5 s

6 s

Black Rk.

5 6

Shag Rk.
166

CARRICK NATH PT.
IRIA 2 m 30 sec.
H.W. 2 2 m 5 sec.

St ANTHONY HD.
IRIA sec.

Osqo.

5 5
white

red

white

Water Tr.

St MAWES Harbour

Porthcuel R.

Trethom Cr.

R. FAL

See Chart No 47

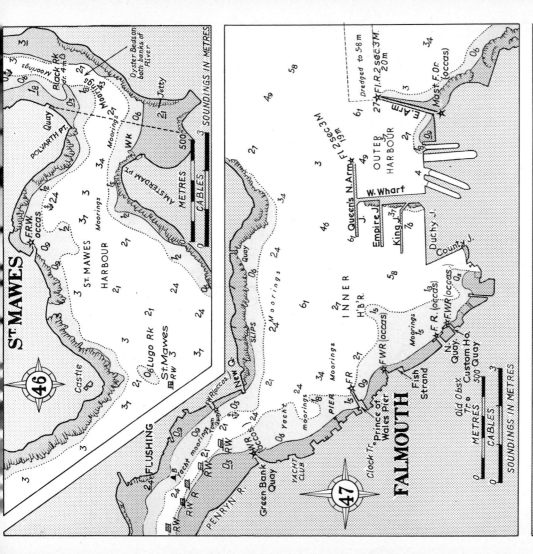
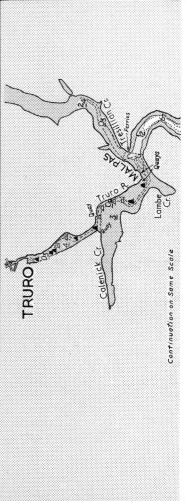

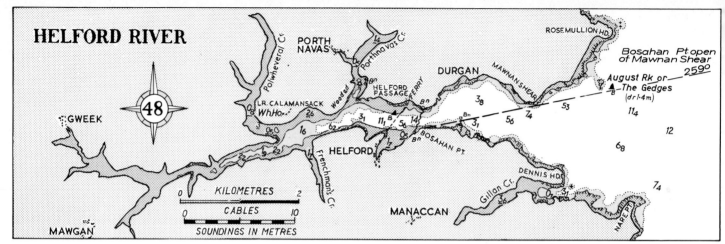

HELFORD RIVER

ROSEMULLION HD.

Bosahan Pt open
of Mawnan Shear ————259°

PORTH
NAVAS

Porthnavas Cr.

DURGAN

August Rk or
——The Gedges
(dr 1·4m)

MAWNAN SHEAR

Polwheveral Cr.

48

HELFORD
PASSAGE

Bn

3_8

5_3

11_4

GWEEK

LR. CALAMANSACK
WhHo.

Wooded

FERRY

Bn

$2·6$

$1·6$

6_2

3_1

11_1

5_6

14

Bn

7_4

5_6

12

6_8

HELFORD

Bn

0_5

BOSAHAN PT.

3_1

7_4

Frenchmans Cr.

$2·5$

$0·9$

$1·6$

KILOMETRES   2

CABLES   10

SOUNDINGS IN METRES

DENNIS HD.

Gillan Cr.

5_6

MANACCAN

NARE PT.

MAWGAN

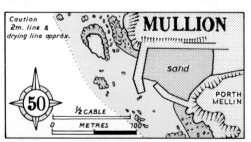

0_4

100 METRES
½ CABLE

4_7

0_4

0_4

0 dr.

0 dr.

dr.

49

sand

DOLOR PT.

COVERACK

0 F.S.

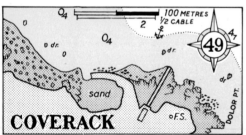

Caution
2m. line &
drying line approx.

MULLION

sand

50

½ CABLE

METRES   100

PORTH
MELLIN

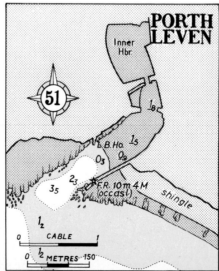

PORTH
LEVEN

Inner
Hbr.

51

1_8

1_5

L.B.Ho.

0_3

0_9

2_3

3_5

☆ FR. 10m 4M
(occasl)

shingle

1_2

0 CABLE   1

0 ½ METRES 150

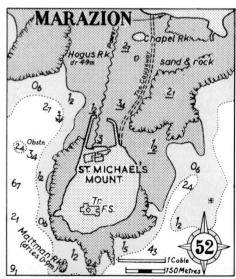

MARAZION

Chapel Rk

Hogus Rk
dr 4·9m

sand & rock

2_1

The Causeway

0_6

1_2

1_2

2_7

3_4

1_2

Obstn

2_4

3_4

1_2

1_2

0_6

6_7

ST MICHAELS
MOUNT

2_4

2_1

0_6

Tr.
F.S.

1_2

Maltman Rk
(dries 0·9m)

1_2

1_5

4_3

52

9_1

1 Cable

150 Metres

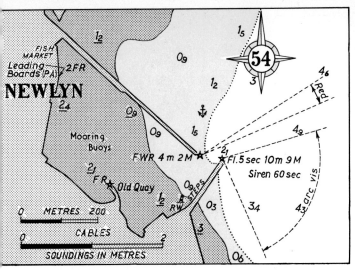
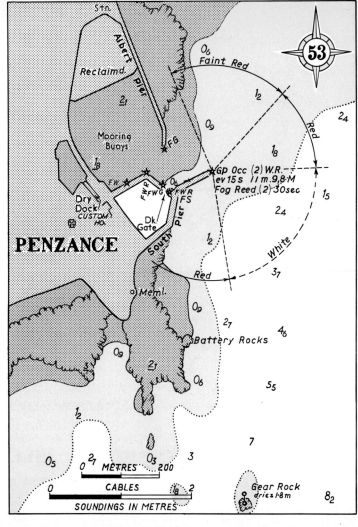
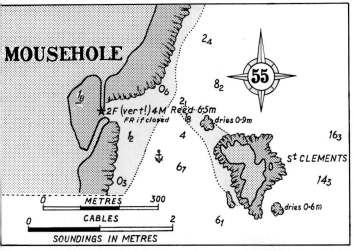

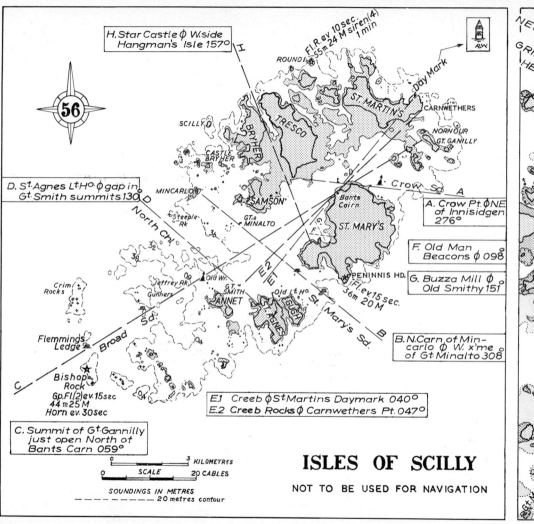
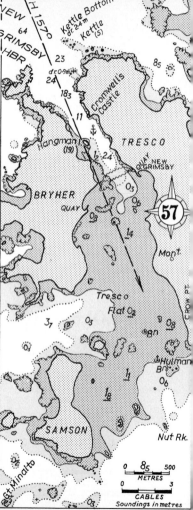

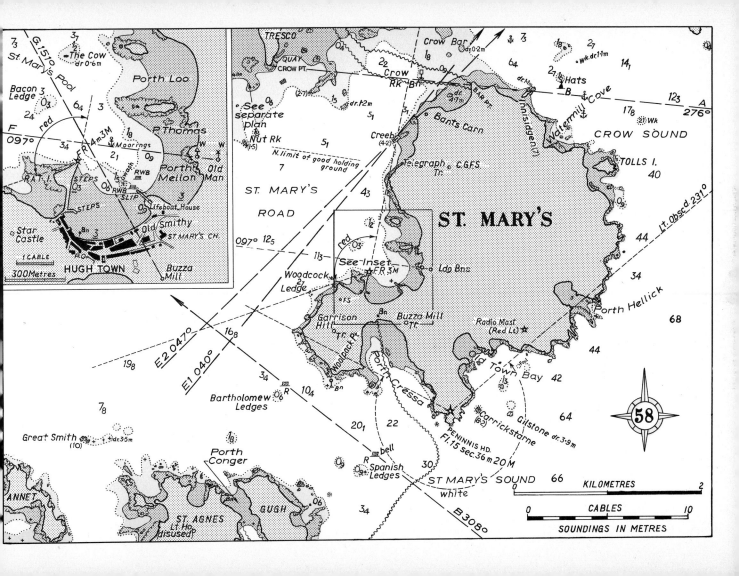

NOTES